To D

May God continue to grant you His Gift of Joy now and throughout your life. God bless!

The Joy of Being a
DEACON

Deacon John F.

The Joy of Being a
DEACON

JOHN P. FLANAGAN

Resurrection Press
An Imprint of
CATHOLIC BOOK PUBLISHING CO.
Totowa • New Jersey

First published in June, 2016 by Resurrection Press, Catholic Book Publishing Corporation.

ISBN 978-1-933066-18-9

(T-RP764)

Printed in USA

1 2 3 4 5 6 7 8 9

www.catholicbookpublishing.com

DEDICATION

I wish to dedicate this book The Joy of Being a Deacon *to all Permanent Deacons worldwide. May your joy increase as you continue to labor in the vineyard of the Lord. And may you always remember that the Sacrament of Holy Orders confers upon you a special grace as well as an indelible, sacramental character or "seal" by which you share in the priesthood of Christ as you carry out your ministry for the greater honor and glory of God.*

Acknowledgments

I THANK Monsignor Gregory Vaughan, pastor of the Church of St. Catharine, for the privilege of continuing to serve under his able leadership; Monsignor Eugene M. Rebeck, former pastor of St. Catharine with whom I served during his 28-year tenure and experienced his spiritual guidance and wisdom. I am also grateful to serve with my fellow parish deacons Thomas DiCanio, Christopher Hansen, and Michael Lonie. To my good friend Deacon James Walsh for his invaluable advice and counsel.

Most Reverend David M. O'Connell, C.M., JCD, Bishop of Trenton, New Jersey Diocese

Very Reverend Bishop Robert F. Morneau, D.D. Auxiliary Bishop Emeritus for the Diocese of Green Bay, Wisconsin; Pastor of Resurrection Catholic Church, Green Bay, WI

Reverend John Catoir, J.C.D., Founder and President of the St. Jude Media Ministry; Former Director of the Christophers

I am especially grateful to Lillian Nadler for the countless hours she dedicated to editing this manuscript; to Jill Thoms who patiently and joyfully typed and re-typed the many drafts; Dana Olore for her technical advice and Deacon Chris Hansen, the computer guru par excellence.

Contents

Foreword

As BISHOP, I am frequently asked to review manuscripts composed by people throughout my Diocese. I receive many texts written on a variety of topics, usually spiritual or theological, more than I could possibly read with the interest and enthusiasm that their authors evidence and expect. I must confess, it is not a task that I relish, given the multiple responsibilities that fill my day. And, so, when I received this manuscript from Deacon John Flanagan, I agreed to read it but cautioned that I might not get to it right away. I waited until a Sunday afternoon in late summer when I had some time to spare and opened up the pages you now have before you.

What I discovered was a delightful meditation on joy, carefully written and containing the reflections of a man, one of my deacons, about his life and ministry. Every page, in fact, every paragraph led me to think about my own life and ministry as a source of grace and joy. I read the text from cover to cover in a single sitting and found myself wishing for more. Honest, humorous, encouraging and poignant were the adjectives that immediately came to mind as I put down the pages. This book filled me with joy because that was exactly what it was intended to do. I wanted to cheer out loud and place this book in the hands of every deacon and priest that I knew as soon as possible. It was not simply good. It was compelling and, I hope, contagious.

John Flanagan's *The Joy of Being a Deacon* is an easy read because it is a great read. It presents an experience of several decades of ministry that confirms the real joy of saying "yes" to God. Anyone who wishes to pursue a call, a vocation, or who wants to look back on having done so, cannot help but sense the fulfillment and joy that comes with opening one's heart to the Lord! As St. Augustine once said, *"Tolle et Lege,"* pick up and read!

Most Reverend David M. O'Connell, C.M., J.C.D.
Bishop of Trenton

Introduction

"YOU will show me the path to life; you will fill me with joy in your presence and everlasting delights at your right hand" (Ps 16:11).

It is said that some books have hearts and souls in their message and production. In this book on joy I hope to reveal the heart and soul of the deacon and his life as servant-leader as well as one of love and joy. These first two gifts of the Holy Spirit are joined together in our ministry. We can't have one without the other.

When Emilie Cerar of the Catholic Book Publishing Corp., invited me to write this book about the joy in the diaconate I was both delighted and fully aware of the need to present a realistic portrayal of the deacon's life. It gave me the opportunity to publicly proclaim in print what we, as deacons, have always known and experienced but may not have always expressed. We really do find genuine joy as servants and leaders as we minister to others. In communicating this message of love and joy I committed my heart and soul to the task because I believe so intensely in the role of the diaconate and the imperative to proclaim the "Good News" with enthusiasm.

This book on joy is not a text on "How to Be a Deacon." It is about joy, love, and the lifetime commitment of all permanent deacons, married, single, widowed and retired, who experience the normal difficulties in life but possess that special spiritual joy and love as they minister as servant-leaders in their communities. Those retired deacons who "have borne the heat of the day," as well as those aging veterans who are "rounding third and headed for home," will discover their inner joy of service renewed as they peruse these pages.

The message in this book is also directed to those men considering enlisting in the permanent diaconate. They will discover an extensive description of the deacon's life with its struggles, obligations, and achievements, but above all, the inner peace, joy, and rewards which the typical deacon experiences in his day-to-day ministry. The deacon candidate will join a growing army of committed deacons and servants. As of 2014 CARA (Center for Applied Research on the Apostolate) reports there are 42,104 permanent deacons worldwide; 17,104 in the United States and another 2,018 in various stages of preparation. May their tribe increase!

No one has a monopoly on spiritual joy and certainly the Clergy and Religious do not have exclusive rights to this gift of the Holy Spirit. Pope Francis, in his encyclical "The Joy of the Gospel," *(Evangelii Gaudium)* writes, "No one is excluded from joy brought by the Lord." All then who read this book can learn how to possess joy in their own lives. I do focus, however, on the special opportunities deacons are given to develop joy in their various ministries. I also identify the methods to cultivate that special joy as well as the dangers that may destroy it.

Spiritual joy is distinctly different from the conventional concept of happiness. Happiness depends on what happens in our lives, as well as those circumstances, people, and events over which we often have little or no control. It is fleeting and usually short term in nature. Real joy, however, is that constant, abiding, and personal relationship with God that we experience when we do His will as loving servants. This joy may often be expressed in various outward ways through our enthusiastic demeanor, laughter, humor, and cheerful attitude. To be joyful does not mean we become clowns, buffoons, or comedians. But we still can be identified as "Fools for Christ."

St. Paul writes in 1 Corinthians 4:10 "We are fools for the sake of Christ, but you are wise in Christ. We are weak but you are strong." Paul does not say we are foolish because we follow Christ's teachings, but we may appear so and be ridiculed by non-believers. St. Ignatius of Loyola adds laughter to Paul's narrative when he tells his followers, "Out of gratitude and love then, we should desire to be recounted as fools, laugh and grow strong."

You will discover in this book the many ways in which the deacon derives joy in his life and ministry. But there is one source, that above all, is paramount and it is the main message of this book. It is the deep and abiding relationship with God and the love of the Holy Eucharist. The Real Presence is not only the "Source and Summit" of our faith but the most powerful source of spiritual grace and joy.

"It is a fount of joy, which enables us to receive everything from the hand of God and contemplate His presence in everything and everyone" (Pope Francis, Address to the 66th Assembly of the Italian Episcopal Conference, May 14, 2014).

A DEACON'S PRAYER

O Lord Jesus Christ, I have answered Your call to be a servant to all. Although I am unworthy, yet You have called me by name. Increase in me the spirit of love and joy as I minister to others; teach me to share that love and joy with all without reservation.

Instruct me in the way I should go by granting me the wisdom to know Your will, the courage to accept it, and the power to do it.

Grant me the humility to recognize the truth in who I am.

Direct me to follow Your example as a true servant-leader by serving the needs of others and leading them to You.

Inspire me to use the talents I have received without any desire for public recognition and always for the greater honor and glory of God.

Above all, help me to be grateful for the privilege of receiving You in the Holy Eucharist, my greatest source of grace, strength, and joy. Amen.

—J. P. F.

Chapter 1

HOW HUMOR AND LAUGHTER ARE EXPRESSIONS OF JOY

"A cheerful heart is good medicine but a downcast spirit dries up the bones."   Prov 17:22

Do deacons experience enough genuine joy, humor, and laughter in their ministry? This question may seem needless to most of us. To others it may appear frivolous. But I take humor in ministry very seriously. Joy must play an important role in our ministry or we are missing out on a major part of our vocation.

I think most of us would agree that when we use humor judiciously, we improve our relations with all whom we serve. Many saints, theologians, and spiritual writers throughout the centuries have asserted that the God-given gifts of laughter and humor are essential to a healthy spiritual existence. Humor is also a healing agent, helping us gain humility and see the truth in ourselves.

What the Saints Say about Humor

Saint Philip Neri (1515-1595), founder of the Oratory Order, who could be called the Patron Saint of humor, began his morning prayer, "A joke a day and I'm on my way, with no fear of tomorrow." He was known for his evangelical simplicity and joyous service to God. His joyful attitude did more to attract people to Christ than any other talent. While I am not suggesting we take our diaconal duties less seriously, we should recall that our joyful demeanor reaffirms our commitment to Christ's teachings and communicates to others how we rejoice in the "Good News." Ours is not a morose and gloomy religion, but a triumphant one. I love Saint Teresa of Avila's comment, "From somber devotions and sour-faced saints, good Lord deliver us."

Surprisingly, St. Thomas Aquinas, a Doctor of the Church, wrote, "It is requisite for the relaxation of the mind that we make use, from time to time, of playful deeds and jokes." And later he wrote, "no one can live without joy."

In the Middle Ages, St. Bernard, Abbot of the Cistercian Monastery in Clairvaux, France, and founder of 163 monasteries, ordered that a special session called "Jucunda," meaning humor hour, also known as "playful devotions" be scheduled as part of monastic routine. He realized that all prayer and no play make monks dull fellows. St. John Chrysostom, the Golden Mouth, announced that, "Laughter has been implanted in our soul that the soul may sometimes be refreshed."

What Theologians and Spiritual Writers Say about Joy and Laughter

"Humor is the prelude to faith and laughter is the beginning of prayer." Reinhold Niebuhr, Theologian

Normally we consider theologians to be austere, serious individuals, preoccupied with the systematic and rational study of religion and spirituality. Humor, generally, is not their forte. I remember attending an annual retreat conducted by the dean of the theology department at a major seminary. We expected several days of dull, boring, theological dissertations. Instead, his eyes glowed with joy and excitement as he opened the "good news" of Sacred Scripture.

Theologian Karl Barth elevated the dignity of laughter when he wrote, "Laughter is the closest thing to the grace of God." Soren Kierkegaard followed up when he proclaimed, "Humor is intrinsic to Christianity." Reinhold Niebuhr adds, "Laughter is the beginning of prayer." Martin Luther concludes, "You have as much laughter as you have faith." He humorously adds, "If you are not allowed to laugh in heaven I don't want to go there."

The Role of Humor in the History of the Church

"No one can live without joy."   St. Thomas Aquinas

When we look back into the history of the Church, we may be surprised to learn the theological emphasis was on the divinity of Christ rather than His humanity. The liturgical focus was on sin, penance, damnation, and hell. Both clergy and the faithful alike concentrated on the passion, crucifixion, and death of Christ. The Resurrection of Christ received less emphasis.

It seemed the Church, more often, frowned on laughter and humor as sacrilegious and a ridicule of religious beliefs. Pope Leo I the Great, Pontifex Maximus (440-461) was well named. He negotiated peace with the Hun and thus saved Rome. He started the practice of private confession and forbade nuns to marry but he also prohibited priests from using jokes in homilies. It was ironic that he was succeeded by Pope Hilarion, whose name means "the joyful or smiling one."

There followed a long line of saints who took a dim view of laughter. For example, St. Ambrose wrote, "Joking should be avoided even in small talk." St. Basil follows up with, "Christians ought not to laugh nor even suffer laughmakers. Finally, Clement of Alexandria offered, "avoid humorous and unbecoming words."

I wonder what they would think about Jesus having a good laugh with His friends. I doubt they would approve of my humor, bad as it is at times, or that of my deacon colleagues. Even the great St. Augustine disapproved of humor in general, but conceded, "There could be some joking from time to time." Then St. Francis Assisi came along with his joyful attitude that won thousands to the joy of the Gospel, and his joyous spirituality continues to influence millions today.

Fr. James Martin, S.J., author of *Between Heaven and Mirth*, addressed a recent Deacon's Convocation, speaking on humor and the saints. Afterwards, I shared with him a quotation that is supposed to have been part of an ordinance of the Second Council of Constance (1414): "If any cleric or monk speaks jocular words such as provoke laughter, let him be anathema." We both doubted its authenticity. Fr. Martin researched it and discovered that it was, in fact, apocryphal. We both were relieved.

Fortunately, in the past century our Church leaders have come to realize that focusing solely on the suffering and sober aspects of our faith represented an unbalanced theology. It was contrary to the Good News message of the Gospel. We are both suffering servants as well as children of the Resurrection. Fr. Martin, who observed that "humor is not all that highly valued in the Catholic Church today," probably surprised his audience at the recent meeting of the National Federation of Priests' Councils when he said, "If you are deadly serious all the time, you are probably spiritually dead." Perhaps that might apply to some of us at times, as well.

Humor and Laughter in the Bible

"Once more I will fill your mouth with laughter and your lips with rejoicing."   Job 8:2

There are 27 to 42 references to humor and laughter in Sacred Scripture depending on the interpretations of various biblical scholars. In addition the word joy or its equivalent appears 287 times. Of course, I am not about to cite them all here but Sarah's story you should enjoy. It begins already in the book of Genesis. Listen to this conversation between God and Sarah: "So Sarah laughed to herself and said, 'Now that I am so withered and my husband is so old, am I still to have sexual pleasure? But the Lord said to Abraham, 'Why did Sarah laugh and say, 'Shall I really bear a child, old as I am?' Is there anything more marvelous for the Lord to do? At the appointed time, about this time next year, I will return to you, and Sarah will have a son?' Because she was afraid, Sarah lied saying, 'I didn't laugh.' But he said, 'Yes you did'" (Gen 18:12-15). Then Sarah's husband, Abraham, had his turn: "Then Abraham fell on his face and laughed, and said in his heart, 'Shall a child be born to a man who is one hundred years old?'" (Gen 17:17, KJV). Naturally, they named their son Isaac, which means "son of laughter."

Did Christ Ever Laugh or Demonstrate Humor?

"Let me be more provocative and suggest that thinking about Jesus without a sense of humor may be close to heresy."   Fr. James Martin, S.J.

In his book, *The Sense of Humor in Scripture*, Rev. Lee van Rensburg writes, "Over the past two decades, more and more scholars have given serious attention to seeking out the presence and function of humor in the Old and New Testaments and particularly in the life and ministry of Christ." Henri Cornier, in his book, *The Humor of Jesus*, comments that exegetes and theologians now agree through their literary research that Christ indeed used many types of humor in His teachings. Furthermore, in no way should this discovery eclipse our reverence for the salvific message of the Gospel. All this having been said—should we laugh more in our ministry? Certainly! Because joy, humor, and laughter are a vital part of our diaconal life.

Did Christ ever laugh? Of course He did! Basic logic would tell us that, but still many Catholics are reluctant to connect humor to Christ and His teachings. It runs counter to their perception of Jesus. For years, I displayed in our deacons' office a portrait of "The Risen Christ by the Sea of Galilee"— laughing because He defeated Satan and conquered death. Most of my visitors, upon gazing at it would smile in approval. Some would challenge it by asking if I could show them in the Bible where it stated that Christ ever laughed. My response: "That omission doesn't mean He didn't." After all, laughter is more frequent than tears and laughter is a universal connector since everyone laughs. Laughter is an outward expression of inner joy. Father McSweeney, Director of the Christophers, wrote, "I am convinced that the ability to laugh, especially at ourselves, is a Divine gift."

The Bible cites three instances when Christ wept: He wept over Jerusalem; He wept at the death of Lazarus (Jn 11:35); and He offered "loud cries and tears" (Heb 5:7). If He shed tears as a man then it follows that surely He laughed. He is both human and divine with all the attributes of humanity.

To deny His sense of humor is to deny His humanity. Can we imagine little children approaching a grouchy Jesus when He invited them to come to Him (cf. Mk 10:14)? How could He attract disciples to follow Him and the people to listen to Him if He appeared as a dour and humorless individual?

The Laughing Christ

"But take courage, I have overcome the world."

Jn 16:33

The portrait "The Risen Christ by the Sea" which I kept in our deacons' office has become tremendously popular among Christians of all denominations. It is displayed in numerous churches, parish centers, religious schools, and retreat centers throughout the U.S.

It has been called, "The Easter Laugh," signifying a depiction of Christ's last laugh at the devil; "The Laughing Jesus" and "The Joyful Jesus." It is prominently displayed on Holy Humor Sunday, a celebration of joy over the resurrection of Christ celebrated by a growing number of churches on the second Sunday after Easter. Its history is most interesting. Father Martin Clarks, a former chaplain in the New York police department, asked his friend and artist, Jack Jewell, to paint a representation of a smiling, risen Christ. Jewell's gift has impressed millions through the years and epitomizes the reality that we Christians are a joyful resurrection people despite living in Good Friday times.

What Deacons Give Up

"He is no fool who gives up what he cannot keep to gain what he cannot lose."   Richard Elliott

Deacons have given up little to gain much. We are discovering the real secret of joy in service to others. We experience the satisfaction and joy that we are fulfilling our call. We take life and ministry seriously but not ourselves. We pray that when we hear Christ's final call it will be: "Well done good and faithful servant..." (Mt 25:21).

Chapter 2

AN INVITATION TO JOY

"Introibo Ad Altare Dei, ad Deum qui laetificat juventutem meam."

"I will go unto the altar of God, to God who gives joy to my youth."   Ps 43:4

(Altar server's response to the celebrant's opening prayer in the former Latin Mass.)

This book is about joy...that special joy that deacons experience as they serve God and His people. I define the word or concept of joy in its authentic scriptural sense. Joy is the second fruit of the Holy Spirit. Unlike the concept of happiness, which is a temporary emotion, joy is a serene and lasting state of mind and soul. The deacon's primary source of joy is his intimate relationship with God.

Deacons, the world over, travel individual journeys on their way to ordination. Many recognize their calling early and follow a path directly to the diaconate. There are others, like myself, who take detours to their diaconate destination. But once we ascend the Altar of

God and engage in our own individual ministries, we, as the band of deacon brothers, share one precious gift in common, a profound sense of joy as servants of Christ and His people. I would like to share my journey with you that began many years ago.

Planting the Seeds of Service to God

"Train up a boy in the way he should go, even when he is old, he will not swerve from it." Prov 22:6

I believe the seeds of service to God are sown at various stages in a person's life. I first learned about serving God and others upon seeing my mother helping the less fortunate in our neighborhood. When I was about seven or eight years old, I saw her carrying hot meals to our sick and poor neighbors. This sincere act of charity and selflessness motivated me to help her.

Homeless people knocked at our door regularly and mom never refused to feed them. I thought it was a burden for her, but the radiant smile on her face proved otherwise. Our family had very little in the way of financial resources, but mom was always eager to share. I didn't realize it then but the seeds of giving, sharing, and serving were gradually taking root in my heart.

Most dioceses require a candidate to have demonstrated a history of service in his parish as one of the conditions of acceptance into the diaconate formation program. Like myself, most deacons I know have a history of helping people for years before they considered a vocation to the diaconate. This impulse to help others seems to be an integral part of a deacon's character.

The First Formal Invitation to Serve Christ— The Altar Server

Sister Mary Teresa, my fourth grade teacher, startled us one morning when she announced, "Boys, if any of you are interested in training to become altar servers, you may sign up after class. Bishop Guilfoyle will teach you the Latin prayers during the next eight Saturdays, but I will give you the final examination." We loved the bishop because he reminded us of the popular actor, Bing Crosby, when he played the role of Father O'Malley in the film, "Going My Way." He was a favorite among both the adults and kids because he always greeted everyone with a smile. If he saw you smiling he would call you *Beatus Vir* meaning "Happy Man." He coached our junior baseball team and bought us ice cream whether we won or lost our game.

I signed up immediately and Bishop Guilfoyle taught us well. He reassured us that it was an honor to participate with the priest on the altar at Mass, and I was very excited at the prospect of enjoying this privilege. Becoming an altar server and having a part-time job were "rites-of-passage" in the Catholic culture of that day. Like most youths, I knew the responses by heart, and I felt confident when I took the examination.

Some days after the exam the results were posted on the Cathedral School front door. Despite a heavy snowstorm, I raced five blocks to the school where some of my buddies were already congratulating one another. I scanned the posted list of those who passed. John Flanagan's name was missing. "There had to be a big mistake," I thought. "I failed the Bishop and myself." I tried to hide my salty tears which began to flow freely as I silently slinked away from the winners. I shouted to God on the way home, "This is a big deal! I wanted so much to serve You, but You let me down."

Six months later, with Mom's encouragement, I retook the exam and passed. Being present with the priest on the altar and witnessing the miracle of changing the bread and wine into the Body and Blood of Christ was always an awesome experience. Another seed was sown: the beginning of a friendship with Christ and a certain sense of joy that seemed to grow each time I served at the altar of the Cathedral of the Blessed Sacrament.

My initial altar server rejection bothered me for a long time. Perhaps it was my boyhood pride or the negative comments from my pals, but most of all the question, "If God wanted me to serve, why did He sometimes make it so difficult?"

In retrospect, the event seems so minor, but to a lad of only nine years it was a huge heartbreak. It was really a blessing in disguise as it began to prepare me for many future rejections both in my secular life and in my diaconate ministry. Above all, these experiences brought me the gifts of patient perseverance and ultimately, joy.

Even today (forty years later), despite how I might feel when I go unto the altar of God, I experience an unusual sense of serenity and peace. Problems disappear...it's time to worship with joy! Most deacons confirm they also have a similar experience.

A peak reward came when Bishop Guilfoyle invited my brother Joe and me to serve at his Mass in the private Cathedral Chapel. Most altar boys I knew were not angels. We fooled around before and after Mass, but (for the most part) on the altar we were well behaved. Besides, God and Sister Mary Teresa were watching. My mom sometimes called us "Church Angels and Street Devils." Just being on the altar transformed us.

The Second Invitation—The Diaconate

"Do not worry about anything, but present your needs to God in prayer...."   Phil 4:6

Years later, four of us had just finished teaching religious education classes for seventh and eighth-grade boys when our pastor announced quite matter-of-factly, "Gentlemen, I'm inviting you to consider doing something even greater and more permanent for God and the Church." He had our instant attention. "Bishop

George Ahr, our current Bishop of the Trenton, New Jersey Diocese, has implemented the Permanent Diaconate, an ancient level of Holy Orders. I would like you to think about attending an information session and learn about becoming a Permanent Deacon." When he left we looked at each other in surprise; discussed it briefly, and unanimously decided we were not interested.

Months later, Jerry Henwood, a deacon candidate, approached me at a Charismatic Prayer Meeting and whispered, "John, why are you reluctant? Why not follow through with your pastor and go to the orientation meeting?" The next day I approached the pastor, "Father" I began, "I've changed my mind. I really would like to find out more about the Diaconate Program." His reply shocked me like a taser jolt: "Well John, I really wasn't thinking about you when I made that invitation." "That settles that...It's not my calling...After all, I'm used to rejection," I said to myself and put the idea on the backburner.

Deacon Jerry, however, didn't give up so easily and invited me and my wife to be his guests at the next Diaconate Orientation. After listening to the role of a Permanent Deacon and his lifetime commitment, my wife Eileen and I both agreed that I should consider serving God in other ways, since I did not believe that I would be accepted. Jerry and the Holy Spirit had other ideas and soon our new pastor suggested that I become a deacon. So, despite several setbacks, I entered the program and was ordained a Permanent Deacon on May 16, 1981.

In the Book of Samuel 3:5-8 the Lord called Samuel three times and he responded by going to Eli who finally agreed it really was God who was calling him to be a leader. In a certain sense I was invited three times, and my previous rejections discouraged me, but in the end God was doing the calling and God got His way.

Who is Worthy?

"You did not choose me. Rather, I chose you. And I appointed you to go out and bear fruit..."   Jn 15:16

It is not unusual for a candidate preparing for the Permanent Diaconate to comment, "I'm really not worthy." Our Director finally squelched that false modesty by categorically stating, "No candidate for the Priesthood or Permanent Diaconate is worthy to be ordained. Only God's grace will prepare you, so let's get on with our chosen mission."

I was always intrigued by how many different ways deacon candidates receive the call to serve and how diverse their backgrounds are. The wife of one of my deacon candidate classmates once cleverly said, "You guys are like a rag-tag army, but you all have one thing in common: You all are consumed with a passion and joy to serve Christ." To that comment I respond "Amen."

God's Ways Are Not Our Ways

Some preachers are fond of comparing the Apostles' qualifications to be Christ's followers with modern recruiting criteria. Their conclusion: The Apostles would never make the cut today. I believe these preachers missed the point.

In my various business careers I hired a goodly number of people but terminated only a few. "Fire in the belly" or tons of enthusiasm was the prime qualification that I was seeking. Experience and education came in second and third respectively. The latter two are necessary for deacons, but the passion to serve, or enthusiasm for Christ's ministry is an absolute requirement because this is what produces fruit.

When it comes to worthiness, I recall the Christian journalist Sherwood Wirt citing an approach that southern preacher Samuel Porter Jones used in inviting people to Christ. One evening at a prayer meeting, Jones invited a man to come to Jesus but the individual replied, "No Sir, I ain't fittin." Jones then said "Come up here and get fittin." The nervous gentleman insisted, "I ain't fittin to get fittin." Preacher Jones finally said, "Let me tell you that the very fact that you don't feel "fittin" is the very thing that commends you to God."

A veteran vocation director when asked the question by prospective seminary candidates, "Father, how will I really know if I have a vocation?" responded, "When you feel a sense of joy with your decision you will know." Let me assure my brother deacons and those considering the diaconate that the fact you may feel unworthy is not only a sign of humility but a signal that endears you to Christ and an invitation to follow Him and experience a sense of joy with your decision.

Discerning God's Calling—What Is God's Plan for Me?

"For I know well the plans I have in mind for you says the Lord, plans for your welfare not your woe."
Jer 29:11

Spiritual writers, theologians, and the Gospel message all remind us that when we know and follow God's plan as it is revealed to us, then we are doing His will and will experience true joy. In his book *The Joy of Full Surrender*, Jean Pierre de Caussade, S.J. reinforces this belief when he writes, "The secret of sanctity and happiness rests in one's fidelity to the will of God as it presents itself in the duty of the present moment."

Let me share with you the story of a man who unequivocally accepted God's plan and was happy. As part of the diaconate selection process, our diocese would assign a deacon to interview candidates. I was once given this task to talk to an aspirant named Harold. The session turned out much differently than I expected. Harold was a Wall Street executive, who was very active in his parish and also financed a food bank in his community.

Like the Marines' recruitment slogan: "We Are Looking For A Few Good Men," I knew Harold was the kind of man for whom we were looking. He seemed to be the ideal candidate. I asked Harold the final question of the interview, "What would be your reaction Harold, if the Diaconate Office did not accept you into the Program?" Without hesitation he replied, "John, I would willingly accept their decision as the will of God. I would, of course, be disappointed but I would continue to be happy in doing my current ministry." Harold gave the perfect answer! Eventually, he was not accepted into the Deacon Formation Program, but he continued his ministry feeding the hungry and housing the homeless. Harold died six months later. May his tribe increase.

Ordination

*"This is the day the Lord has made, let us rejoice
and be glad in it."*   Ps 118:24

The years of training were finally over. The Cathedral was packed with family and friends who had come to witness their spouse, son, brother, or friend receive this sacrament. The Deacon's spouse and pastor help vest him with the stole, a sign of the Order of Diaconate and the dalmatic, a symbol of servanthood. The joyful hymns of the choir are deafening and the thunderous peals of the organ add to the solemnity.

The deacon candidates prostrate themselves on the floor of the aisle or altar as a sign of humility. Later each candidate kneels before the Bishop who extends his hands over the candidate and sings or says aloud the Prayer of Consecration. The candidate is now an ordained permanent deacon.

The joy and excitement are palpable. This liturgy is celebrated in most dioceses throughout the U.S. on a yearly basis. The ordained deacon has vowed obedience to his Bishop and commitment to Christ for time and eternity. The mood of the deacons on that day is one of exquisite joy. It might best be expressed in Acts 2:4: "All of them were filled with joy and the Holy Spirit."

Opportunities for Humility

While it is true that deacons receive the special sacramental grace of ordination, they still remain human and not angels. Pride of new position and role is the antithesis of the deacon's mission as servant. Opportunities for humility will continue throughout his years of ministry.

When the Pastor Fr. Frank learned that his newly ordained Deacon Earl was becoming unpopular with many of the parishioners because of his haughty attitude, he approached the deacon one day and suggested, "I'd like you to join me on Good Friday morning as we prostate ourselves an hour on the altar as a sign of penance and humility. Deacon Earl reluctantly agreed but he got the message. There they were lying flat, prone on the altar, when a lone parishioner entered the church, spied the two lying in a prostrate position and figured this was a Good Friday devotion and decided to join them. As he took up a face-down position, Deacon Earl gave him a withering look of annoyance, then whispered to the pastor "Can you believe the nerve of this guy, he thinks he's humble, too."

Humility is truth and the effective deacon-servant will readily recognize his deficiencies and thank God for his talents. Parishioners and others will shy away from the officious, sour-faced, arrogant deacon. Matthew Kelly, the renowned Catholic speaker and author, expresses it well when he writes, "Truth and joy are proportionately linked in our lives. The more we live the truth, the more we experience joy. If you do what you know to be good and true, you will experience joy beyond compare."

Ordinarily, the newly ordained is invited by his pastor to assist him at Mass for the first time after ordination. Although I had much experience in my business life in speaking before audiences, I was visibly nervous at the first Mass. When it came time to announce, "Let us offer each other a sign of Christ's peace," I blurted out, "Our Mass is finished, go in peace."

The pastor turned to me in consternation and then in a good natured manner addressed the congregation, "Deacon John is not yet a day ordained and he is already changing the Mass." At least I knew the word "Peace" was there somewhere.

The worst embarrassment was yet to come. Immediately after that Mass, I began removing the sacred vessels from the credence table. A woman whom I vaguely remembered rushed up and in a loud voice heard by departing parishioners, shouted, "Mr. Flanagan, I am shocked to see you in those vestments, you are the last man in our parish that I think should ever become a deacon."

I quietly replied, "Mrs. Blank, I completely agree. I resisted, but God insisted!" My only consolation was that she rarely came to Church and after that parting shot, I never saw her again. Thus began my diaconate with these sobering events. I consoled myself by recalling a humorous quotation, "Nobody's perfect, I'm nobody, therefore I must be perfect."

After Ordination—Challenge or Crisis

The intense five-year spiritual boot camp was finished. Now the deacon is deployed to the field of ministry. He is now in the trenches. For some deacons these first few years may prove challenging, while others, depending on local circumstances, may consider it a period of crisis in their expected role and identity. For both it is certainly an adjustment period. His original enthusiasm and joyful attitude will be tested frequently. I fell in both of these categories.

Rightful Role and Identity

"It takes time and education of the parishioners about your role here in the parish," cautioned my pastor. "You can't demand respect and recognition, you must first earn it." It's the wise deacon who listens to his pastor's counsel. After all, he has seen his share of spiritual combat and parish politics; and he knows how to minister to God's people. Our parishioners understood that the deacon is not a glorified altar boy or a "wanna-be" priest. He is a member of the clergy, exercising a distinct sacramental role but he is also a servant-leader who is expected to be a cooperative member of the parish ministry team.

Years later, at a Deacon's Conference, the priest coordinator announced, "Now we are opening our session to questions, suggestions, and complaints." The usual comments and suggestions came from the assembly of two hundred deacons and wives. Then a recently ordained deacon stood up to speak, "We don't get enough respect from some priests and parishioners. Sometimes my pastor doesn't let me exercise my rightful role in ministry." He rambled on, to the embarrassment of most of those in attendance. I was sorely tempted to get up and offer a gentle rebuttal, but I resisted against a possible verbal showdown. Later, I spoke to him privately and repeated what my pastor had told me about acceptance. I also added that when we entered the military we took an oath to be loyal to our country and accept the rules and orders of the military service. When we accepted a job, we were expected to conform to the employee's guidelines, and when we were ordained we made a promise of obedience to the Bishop and to our pastor as his representative. He listened and went on to create a unique ministry that has helped thousands. Since deacons are servant-leaders, we are tough spiritual marines who do not mind ministering in the trenches.

Impact of Diaconal Duties on the Family

The inability or reluctance of spouses to honestly communicate with one another is a major cause of discord and even divorce among married couples. The need for the deacon and his wife to effectively communicate is even more critical because of his life-style and commitments to ministry as well as to family. Although there are certain aspects of ministry which the deacon must keep confidential, for the most part, the wife has the right and the deacon has the obligation to apprise his spouse of his schedule, commitments, etc. When he fails to do so he will create resentment and resistance. Likewise, the deacon as father and model to his children should share with them that his love for them is constant, but he also has made a special commitment to Christ and service to the Church. He will try to spend "quality" time with his children. Unfortunately, some deacons fall victim to the "Super-Servant Syndrome" and attempt to minister to everyone but their wives and their children. They will eventually pay a price for this neglect and may win many battles, but lose the war and jeopardize their joy in the diaconate and with their family.

Time Commitment to Ministry—Performing the Balancing Act

Most deacons have full-time jobs which require that they need to balance the needs of their families, secular careers, and the duties of the diaconate. We are now performing Baptisms, assisting at one or more Sunday Masses, preparing and preaching homilies, conducting pre-nuptial sessions and solemnly witnessing marriages. We also conduct wake services, assist at funeral Masses and conduct cemetery committals. In addition, many deacons are engaged in hospital and nursing home visits, counseling, prison ministry, and other pastoral activities. Parishioners often approach us with situations which, in their minds, would be too embarrassing to discuss with a priest. We go to places to minister where normally most priests do not go. In this manner we complement the priest's role and act as a vital team member.

I am constantly impressed with our brother deacons who live the single life in the unmarried or widowed state. By and large these men seem to dedicate an enormous amount of their time to diaconal ministry. For many, full-time diaconal duties become their life. They are an inspiration to us all. Like most deacons, they receive no salary and work for the glory of God. Then there are those deacons eligible for retirement who wish to remain in the saddle of service. The mandatory retirement age for deacons and priests is usually seventy-five in most dioceses, age seventy in a few. There are those who elect to continue in ministry, with faculties' permission from their bishop and pastor. These men have my greatest admiration since theirs is no small sacrifice.

For some men, the additional responsibilities in the early years of their diaconate can be so overwhelming that the joy of service can begin to disappear. They confuse the urgent with the important. Identifying priorities becomes a challenge. I used to teach time management courses at the American Management Association in New York City and in the various companies at which I was employed. So I decided that if this training helped make profits for those companies, why not help deacons manage their time more profitably for God. I then wrote the book, *Managing Your Time, Energy and Talent in Ministry*, and subsequently taught a time management program to deacon candidates for several years. I was delighted to minister to my brother deacons. I was very much aware that I also needed to practice what I preached, wrote, and taught.

The Ministry Contract or Covenant

Prior to ordination as deacon candidates we are required, in concert with our pastor sponsor, to write a contract or job description of our prospective ministries in the parish. We are urged to identify the needs of our parish that require attention and then determine if we have the requisite skills to minister to those needs. Before meeting with my pastor, I began to consider the Hospital Visitation Ministry. I met with the Hospital Chaplain several times and accompanied him as he made his rounds among the patients. After several weeks he sat me down and said "John, you are not cut out for Hospital Ministry. You lack the bedside manner." I thanked the good Father for his time and patience. I didn't tell him rejection was my sometimes friend. So, when I eventually met with my pastor to discuss my future role, he agreed I should first start an Employment Committee. In a private survey, parishioners told me that next to death and divorce, losing a job caused the most grief in families. That Committee, which helps unemployed parishioners start or restart their job search, is still active after thirty-five years. In addition, we talked about other needs that required help in the parish. "You are missing something very important in your job description, John," he smiled. "I also want you to visit parishioners when they are patients in the hospital." I did the caring ministry for many years and loved it. "Man Proposes...and God disposes."

A deacon's relationship with the community he serves should be a covenant and not simply a contract of service. A contract can be cancelled when one or more of the parties fail to perform, but an authentic servant makes an unconditional commitment regardless of the response or cooperation. A deacon, as servant, should never consider reciprocity, thanks, praise, recognition or a successful outcome as the criteria for his service to others. We all like to receive the above results but should consider it a gift if and when it happens...and not a right we deserve.

Chapter 3

THE SOURCES AND SIGNS OF GENUINE JOY

"I have told you these things so that my joy may be in you and your joy may be complete."   Jn 15:11

"Joy is a sure sign of the Holy Spirit and a foretaste of Heaven."   St. Thomas Aquinas

What is Genuine Joy?

Some spiritual writers and preachers refer to the "secret of joy" acknowledging that the concept is elusive and people have difficulty identifying it. From time immemorial mankind has been seeking true joy but pursuing happiness instead. They yearn to satisfy that deep longing in their hearts but frequently confuse the two emotions. Deacons experience ongoing joy in their ministry as do all those who serve Christ in servanthood.

A simple, yet profound definition of joy is described by Father John Catoir, who is now the President of the St. Jude Media Ministry, as, "Joy is a loving, warm sense of an intimate relationship with God." I firmly believe authentic joy is a spiritual and biblical concept. It is the second of the twelve fruits of the Holy Spirit.

Love is the first. We cannot have joy without love. G.K. Chesterton, a highly acclaimed Catholic writer of the 20th century, expressed it well, "Where love radiates its joy, there we have a feast."

In our modern vernacular and in most languages the words joy and happiness are used interchangeably. They are far from being synonymous in the spiritual sense. Joy can be permanent but happiness is always temporary. "And they lived happily ever after," is a romantic way to end stories, but I prefer to write our life stories as, "We lived joyfully here and in the hereafter." The greatest news is that we can experience both.

Following are some further definitions of joy:

- "Joy is the most infallible sign of the presence of God."—*Leon Bloy*
- "Joy is not an isolated or an occasional consequence of faith; it is an integral part of our whole relationship with God through Christ." —*Reverend Sherwood West*
- "Joy is the echo of God's life within us."—*Joseph Marmion*
- "Joy is a foretaste of eternity."—*Leslie B. Flynn*
- "Joy is not simply a feeling of happiness. Joy is the all-intoxicating feeling of becoming. It is the greatest of emotional and spiritual sensations...we experience joy when we grow, and we grow when we live in the presence of God and listen to the promptings of the Holy Spirit." —*Matthew Kelly*

What Is Happiness?

"Happiness lasts a short time, joy lasts forever; I pray, O Lord, may I have both together." Joyful John

Happiness is one of the most frequently used words in any language. Professor William James, a Harvard University psychiatrist and professor and author of *Varieties of Religious Experience*, defines happiness as, "Life's chief concern....how to gain, how to help, how to recover happiness is for most men the secret of all they do." For most, happiness consists of the pursuit of happiness and the avoidance of pain.

A year ago PBS conducted a world-wide survey asking people what was their greatest desire. Almost ninety percent answered: "I want to be happy." Like most people, I want to be happy. I love weddings, parties, when the Yankees win, when our children do well in life and when the Internal Revenue Service does not bother me.

Recently my friend was on a cruise. He and his wife were very happy until he lost his wallet on board. He became a very unhappy sailor for the rest of his cruise. A while later I lost my wallet and was in a panic, but I finally found it under my bed. I was ecstatically relieved and very happy unlike my friend. The outcome could have been different and often is. There are many events in my life and probably in yours when situations become very disappointing and cause us much unhappiness. Happiness depends on events, people, and circumstances; upon what "happens," over which we usually have little control. But happy events are temporary; once we have experienced them we begin to plan for other pleasurable events. And the cycle continues. Each of us has a "bucket list" of events we want to do because we believe they will make us happy...and they usually do...for a time. If and when the "bucket" is emptied we proceed to fill it again with other potentially pleasurable events. The reality is we will always want more.

The authors of our Declaration of Independence were well advised when they wrote that we are entitled to "Life, liberty and the *pursuit* of happiness." They did not guarantee our happiness nor can anyone else. I am not discouraging the quest for happiness. I believe we are all entitled to some measure of happiness, but we are most certainly entitled to the gift of joy.

In 2012 Hurricane Sandy, later relegated to a super storm being the second costliest in U. S. history, swept up the East coast of the United States, and caused billions of dollars in damage and the loss of lives. Giant waves measuring thirty to forty feet washed houses and watercraft out to sea and destroyed thousands of residences, businesses, and establishments on land. Yet, oceanographers report that despite the terrible turbulence on the ocean's surface, there still existed a serene and undisturbed environment thirty or forty feet below the violent storm above. And so it is with joy. The storms of life may be engulfing us, but when we have true joy deep down in our hearts and souls we will experience peace and serenity. Our bodies, from birth, are genetically programmed for obsolescence, eventually transitioning into "glorified bodies" in eternity. The first part may sound depressing, but the second is thrilling. Imagine that one day your body and mind will be transformed into a perfect being. Yet, we spend billions each year to recapture our youth and renew our bodies simply to delay the inevitable. But the prospect alone that we will live forever in endless joy should reduce our distress over our body's gradual deterioration and our fear of death.

St. Augustine (354-430) who spent a dissolute youth searching for happiness until he converted to the Catholic faith and found true joy in God alone, penned the famous line, "You have made us for yourself O Lord and our hearts are restless until they rest in you." He thus answered the age-old quest for complete happiness, joy, and fulfillment by stating that nothing will fill the incompleteness that we all experience until we have a relationship with God.

Why Priests Are Happy

Msgr. Stephen J. Rossetti wrote a book in 2011 titled *Why Priests Are Happy* which, to date, is arguably the most comprehensive analysis of priests' attitudes about their priesthood. Msgr. Rossetti conducted several surveys in which the main question asked was: "How happy are you in your priesthood?"

In the first survey conducted in 2004 for 1,242 priests from sixteen dioceses in the U.S. over 90% replied that they were very happy. He conducted the second survey in 2009 for 2,482 priests from twenty-three U.S. dioceses and 91.4% agreed they were happy. In similar surveys the results were about the same. In *The Hartford Courant* survey, 94% agreed with the same statement, and *The Los Angeles Times* 2002 survey revealed 90%, while in the National Federation of Priests Council (NFPC) 2001 survey 94% agreed.

Throughout his book, Msgr. Rossetti uses the terms happy and joyful interchangeably. It is apparent in other sections of his surveys that the priest respondents really mean joy in the same sense we describe joy in this book, as the reason for their satisfaction in their priesthood.

So what accounts for the priests' positive response in the surveys? Msgr. Rossetti concludes, "Most importantly, all these secrets of priesthood must be considered secondary to the greatest "secret" of a priest's life and the source of their joy. Again and again these findings highlighted the centrality of the priests' spiritual life for their inner peace, well-being, and personal joy...."

Spirituality Is the Answer for Joy

You may wonder why I included a summary of a survey on priests' attitude to their vocation in this book. I did it because I believe if and when a deacons' survey is conducted the positive results will be similar. Furthermore, although the deacons' role and rank are different from that of priests in the clerical hierarchy, their joy also is primarily a product of their spirituality and close relationship with God.

Why Deacons Are Joyful

Everything I write in this book about the joy of being a deacon may be summarized in one sentence: A deacon's joy flows from his spirituality and close relationship with God.

A priest once remarked to me, "You, as deacons have it both ways, you are permitted through Ordination to administer some of the Sacraments and also to enter the married life." I agree that we are blessed to have many opportunities to serve God and His people and have the additional pleasure of a family life. But we also have our own burdens and responsibilities.

There are many reasons why deacons are and should be joyful, and I try to describe them throughout the various chapters of this book, but this gift of spiritual joy is not exclusive to the clergy. It is available to all who love God. Deacons and priests, however, are blessed with so many occasions to minister and evangelize; consequently, they are presented with numerous opportunities to renew their joy. "To whom much is given much is required." I am almost tempted to advise my brother deacons to practice an eleventh commandment: "You must be joyful and share that joy with others!" The more joy we share with others the more joy we receive from the Holy Spirit. Julian of Norwich, the great English mystic (1342-1423) wrote, "The greatest honor you can give to God is to live in joy because of the knowledge of God's love. If our joy gives honor to God, then it is our duty to be joyful."

Joy in Sacred Scripture

"When I found your words, I devoured them; they became my joy, the happiness of my heart."

Jer 15:16

There are as many as 542 references to joy in the Bible, stretching from the Book of Genesis to Revelation. The Book of Psalms, which has been described as the Book of Joy, contains 105 joyful verses. In fact, in addition to the Liturgy of the Hours, deacons might consider Paul's letter to the Philippians and the Psalms as required reading. When I recite the Liturgy of the Hours, especially in the morning, as all priests and deacons are required to do daily, I get a head start on an attitude of joy for the day because many of the prayers are verses from the Book of Psalms that shout out exhilarating notes of joy.

The Joy of the Gospel

"Your words are what sustain me; they are food to my hungry soul. They bring joy to my sorrowing heart and delight me." *Jer 15:16*

Pope Francis wrote an Apostolic Exhortation in 2014 titled *The Joy of the Gospel (Evangelii Gaudium)*, which is a must read for clergy and laity alike. Pope Francis opens with this declaration: "The joy of the gospel fills hearts and lives of all who encounter Jesus. Those who accept his offer of salvation are set free from sin, sorrow, inner emptiness, and loneliness. With Christ joy is constantly born anew...."

The Pope's book is replete with scriptural references to joy. "The Gospel, radiant with the glory of Christ's cross, constantly invites us to rejoice," the Pope writes. "Rejoice!" is the angel's greeting to Mary (Lk 1:28). Mary's visit to Elizabeth makes John leap for joy in his mother's womb (Lk 1:41). Mary proclaims, "My spirit rejoices in God my Savior" (Lk 1:47). When Jesus begins His ministry, John cries out, "This joy of mine is complete. He must increase, I must decrease" (Jn 3:29-30). His message brings us joy: "I have told you these things so that my joy may be in you and your joy may be complete" (Jn 15:11). Jesus promises His disciples: "You will be sorrowful, but your grief will turn into joy" (Jn 16:20). "I will see you again and your hearts will rejoice, and no one shall deprive you of joy" (Jn 16:22). "The disciples were filled with joy when they saw the

Lord" (Jn 20:20). "And the disciples were filled with joy and with the Holy Spirit" (Acts 13:52).

Pope Francis issues a challenge to all Catholics: "An evangelizer must never look like someone who has just come back from a funeral." I personally admire his direct style. He uses words that both the cab driver and the Cardinal can understand. I chuckled when I heard how he addressed some members of the clergy as "sourpusses." One of his jobs before he entered the Jesuit seminary was as a bouncer in a night club in his hometown in Argentina. I think we can expect more unsettling but straight talk tinged with love and joy from the Supreme Pontiff. Pope St. John XXIII opened wide the windows of the Church to let the fresh air of change rush in; Pope Francis opened them wider to let the sunshine of joy in.

How Do We Increase and Maintain Our Joy?

"Give, and it will be given to you; a good measure, pressed down, shaken together, and running over, will be poured into your lap."   Lk 6:38

Joy is first of all a gift or fruit of the Holy Spirit. Gifts are supposed to be opened and used. Many are often unaware of this and the gift becomes an unclaimed treasure. We should receive it gratefully, accept it humbly and then share our joy with others.

Following are some of the ways we can experience and increase the gift of spiritual joy:

- *Eucharistic Joy*

Receiving the Holy Eucharist at Mass is the most intimate way to experience a joyful relationship with Christ. A non-believer who envied his Catholic friend's belief in the "real presence" of Christ in the Eucharist is reputed to have said, "If I could only believe in that mystery I would crawl on my hands and knees to the altar to receive Christ."

There is the story about St. John Vianney, the Cure of Ars, that is legendary. He kept noticing an elderly parishioner who remained in the church after the daily Mass. The gentleman kept his eyes fixed on the tabernacle and seemed to be in deep meditation. Finally the humble Cure approached and asked the man about his devout action. "I just look at Jesus in the tabernacle and He looks at me, ...and we are happy," he shyly whispered. That's what lovers do. They are just content to look at each other and enjoy the loving relationship. Deacons, especially, are encouraged to attend or participate, when possible, at daily Mass. What a great way to start the day!

- *The Indwelling of the Holy Trinity*

"And I will ask the Father, and he will give you another Advocate to be with you forever, the Spirit of Truth, whom the world cannot accept, because it neither sees him nor knows him. But you know him because he dwells with you, and will be in you" (Jn 14:16-17). This verse from the Gospel of John serves as the basis of the doctrine known as the Indwelling of the Holy Spirit. Jesus then adds, '"Whoever loves me will keep my word, and my Father will love him, and we will come to him and make our abode with Him" (Jn 14:23). It is therefore the entire Holy Trinity, Father, Son and Holy Spirit that dwells within us from the time of our baptism and remains with us as long as we stay in the state of sanctifying grace.

Catholic University scholar Fr. John A. Hardon, S.J., writing about the Divine Indwelling states, "It is the indwelling Trinity, God himself, the uncreated true God living in our souls that makes it possible for us through our knowledge and love to be happy in a way that no one else has a claim to except one in whom God dwells by his uncreated presence of the Holy Trinity. This intimacy with God provides us an indescribable sense of joy."

The problem is that often we are not aware of the stunning reality of God's presence in our soul and the consequent joy we will experience when we are conscious of it. Deacons have an obligation to take advantage of this source of joy and power and share it with others.

• *The Anticipation of Eternal Life*

"I am the resurrection and the life, whoever believes in me, even though he dies, will live, and everyone who lives and believes in me will never die" (Jn 11:25). When doubts about our faith assail us we can take great consolation in this tremendous promise of Christ that we are destined to live forever in eternity.

When deacons emphasize this Gospel message at wakes, Funeral Masses, and cemetery committals we will assuredly give the grieving family and others the most significant gift possible....a gift of hope, love, and joy! They yearn to hear that confirmation that they and their loved ones will one day be reunited forever. Conveying this gospel also renews our joy. In later chapters I will expand on how we can have joy even at times of loss, tragedy, and terminal illness.

• *Trusting God Will Make All Things Right*

"We know God makes all things work together for good for those who love him and who are called according to his purpose" (Rom 8:28). This is one of my favorite promises of Christ. I have adopted it as a daily spiritual mantra, which I silently recite when I begin to feel anxious about completing the duties of the day and my ministry obligations. It helps me put priorities in proper perspective and restores a measure of serenity and joy in my life. Perhaps it will be a boost for you too.

I became so impressed with St. Paul's message that I wrote a yet to be published book titled, *Trusting Love Will Make All Things Right—Stories for Your Spiritual Journey*. I strongly recommend deacons use Romans 8:28 if they ever need to prepare a general or emergency homily. It provides an answer to the many problems people face in their lives. When prayer becomes almost impossible because of our pain, it often helps just to read verses from the Bible like Romans 8:28 and listen to the Word speak to us as we sit in silence.

- *Prayer and Meditation*

"Rejoice always, pray continually; give thanks in all circumstances, for this is the will of God for you in Christ Jesus" (1Thes 5:16-18). It may seem unnecessary to remind deacons to pray without ceasing, since prayers and meditation are part and parcel of the deacon's daily life. Notice Paul prefaces his exhortation with the words, "Rejoice always." Prayer may at times become perfunctory or even difficult but in the end it is guaranteed to produce joy and serenity in our lives.

Knowing God's Will for Us

"...We have not ceased to pray for you and to ask that you may be filled with the knowledge of God's will through all spiritual wisdom and understanding."   Col 1:9

Discovering God's plan for us usually takes considerable patience and prayer. Spiritual advisors suggest we consider the following methods to discern God's plan for our life:

- Prayer—We talk to God about His plan for us.
- Meditation--God talks to us.
- Sacred Scripture—We discover lifetime guidelines.

- Spiritual Direction—It will lead us to proper pathways.
- Spiritual Reading—Affords us valuable insights.
- Consultation with our Confessor—Gives us grace and counsel.
- Soul Friend—Provides a role model we can trust.

When we know and do God's will we are guaranteed a measure of joy which in turn reinforces our desire to persevere in following His plan. "Joy gives strength to do God's will" (Neh 8:10).

Surrendering to God's Will

"There is no spiritual path more secure than that of giving yourself entirely to God."

Jean Pierre de Caussade, S.J.

Surrendering to His will may prove for many of us to be a difficult challenge. Americans typically reject the idea of surrender. We interpret it as failure, giving up, a defeat, and in some instances, tantamount to cowardice. We pride ourselves on being self-sufficient, self-reliant and, above all, totally independent. Spiritual surrender requires we adopt a totally different attitude. Pride is what prevents us from completely abandoning ourselves to God's will, but when we do, an exquisite pervasive joy and sense of contentment is how God will reward us.

A former pastor approached me one day with this request, "John, I want you to periodically attend the

Alcoholics Anonymous meetings conducted on Friday evenings in our parish center." "But, I'm not an alcoholic," I protested. "I know that, but you need to see how people in AA suffer and how you may be called to minister to them."

At the meetings I sat silently, listened attentively, and soon realized that most of the books I read and the seminars I attended about the wisdom of surrendering one's will to God could never teach me as much as witnessing firsthand the real meaning of this commitment.

The men and women at these AA meetings shared how they suffered and caused family and friends to suffer because of their severe addiction. Most testified that surrender to God was their survival. Those in recovery repeatedly declared that turning their lives over to God completely, every day, gave them a joy and peace they had never known before.

Vicarious Joy

Giving consolation and joy to others also gives satisfaction and joy to those who minister. In some form or another the following scene may be repeated every day in hospitals throughout the world. It was one of my first hospital visits to a dying parishioner. Vincent was forty-five, married with children and the owner of several factories. I met his distraught wife outside the door. "Deacon John," she cried, "Vincent is very despondent...he is afraid to die. Can you please pray with him?" I nodded, then entered the room and began to chat and then prayed with Vincent.

Suddenly, he rose up in his bed, grabbed me by my jacket lapels and hoarsely whispered, "John, level with me, man to man, is there really a heaven? Will I ever see my family again?" I then quoted that powerful passage from John 11:25, "I am the resurrection and the life. Whoever believes in me, even though he dies, will live." He relaxed, smiled and said, "Deacon, if what you just quoted proves not to be true, believe me I will certainly come back to haunt you!" Vincent died that night. His wife said he departed a very peaceful man. Incidentally, Vincent has yet to come back to haunt me.

Beware the Thieves of Joy

"Fear not, I am with you; be not dismayed: I am your God. I will strengthen you, and help you, and uphold you with my right hand of justice."

Isa 41:10

There are times in a deacon's life when it seems the joy in ministry has disappeared. The original fervor has faded. Exhaustion and burn-out have taken their toll. Spiritual writers refer to this occupational hazard as acedia, apathy, being lukewarm, or the "dark night of the soul." There are many causes for this malaise. When we forget to embrace the sources of our joy the wellspring will gradually dry up. The two most devious thieves of our joy are fear and worry. Psychiatrists cite the 90/10 rule: Ten percent of patients present legitimate cases of worry; ninety percent complain of imaginary problems or events over which they have no control. Deacons may prove to suffer from needless fear and worry when they take their eyes off the goal and miss the main message in ministry: God is always in control. "Fear not" appears seventy-six times in the Bible. God is sending us a powerful message. When we cultivate spiritual joy we put on the impregnable armor of strength and wield the sword of faith against which the demons of fear and worry are defeated.

I composed the following abbreviated prayer based on St. Paul's letter to the Romans 8:28 and the Serenity Prayer. I try to recite it every morning to establish a positive attitude for the day. "O Lord, give me the wisdom to know Your will, the courage to accept it, and the strength to do it. Amen."

Chapter 4

THE DEACON AS SERVANT-LEADER

"If anyone wishes to be first, he must become the last of all and the servant of all."　　　Mk 9:35

The deacon's mandate and motto might well be: *"Ministrare non ministrari."* Not to be served but to serve. The Marines are proud to be known as "The First to Fight." Deacons should be known as "The First to Serve." Servanthood is our origin, our spiritual heritage, our mandate for ministry and our divine destiny. In this chapter I will focus on the dual role that deacons perform as both servants and leaders and the joy they experience being both.

"If you belonged to the world, the world would love you as its own. But you do not belong to the world because I have chosen you out of the world, and therefore the world hates you" (Jn 15:19). Deacons live and work in the world of business, trades, industry, and commerce. They do not reside in monasteries or rectories, nor do they spend years in seminaries. They wear the clothes or uniforms suitable to their employment situation. They are salesmen, plumbers, lawyers, construction and factory workers, doctors, truck drivers, etc. They come from varied backgrounds. Most are married, some are single, others are widowed or retired. They acquire skills and experience that they then use in their world of ministry. They are called to be servants and leaders in their diaconate role and in many cases to function as servant-leaders in the companies in which they are employed. In writing about the joy of being a deacon I am compelled to share how the concept of servant-leadership operates in both their formal ministry life as well as their occupational work life and how they can derive joy when functioning in both worlds.

What Is Servant-Leadership?

The term Servant-Leader, sounds like an oxymoron, and may seem demeaning to some. It requires the leader to first assume a servant attitude and change from the typical traditional authoritarian manager role to one who encourages feedback, consensus building, and collaboration in lieu of exercising power, position, prestige, coercion, or manipulation among his colleagues or customers. Above all, the authentic servant-leader must possess a deep sense of humility. As Ken Blanchard put it, "Humble leaders don't think less of themselves, they think about themselves less."

Servant-Leadership in Church and Business

"Christ is the greatest leadership model of all times."   Kenneth Blanchard

Servant-Leadership is a relatively new but highly successful management philosophy that hundreds of business executives, Church leaders, and social organizations are now practicing with stunning results. It may well become the preeminent leadership model of the 21st century for business, Church, and society. This prediction is being made by both business and Church authorities throughout the United States. They are literally turning the traditional organizational pyramid upside down. Servant-Leadership, which is an apparent contradictory concept, is dramatically changing the way in which many organizations are conducting their businesses. Above all, this approach promises positive potential for both clergy and laity to more effectively minister to their people.

The origin and history of Servant-Leadership represents an extremely interesting and exciting chapter in the development of management practices in the United States. In 1970 Robert K. Greenleaf, a V.P. of Human Resources with AT&T, launched the modern Servant-Leadership movement with his ground-breaking publication, *The Servant as Leader*. He kept asking the fundamental question posed by his critics, "Can both servant and leader be fused together to become one effective person?" His answer was a definite "Yes," and his life's work to promote this controversial management philosophy and practice began. Speaking at a Convent, he claimed that there was no evidence in the Bible of servanthood. When one nun challenged him, he asked her to identify any passages that spoke about servant-leadership. For such a brilliant scholar, Greenleaf displayed a tremendous vacuum in his research. As we know there are quite a few examples of Christ as servant in the New Testament. At the Wedding Feast of Cana (Jn 2:11) Christ took charge and acted as servant; in Matthew 23:11 Christ exhorted His apostles: "The greatest among you must be your servant." He proclaims in Luke 22:27: "I am in your midst as one who serves." And again in John 13:15 after washing the apostles' feet He reminds them, "I have given you an example. What I have done for you, you should also do."

"Christ is the greatest leadership model of all time." Ken Blanchard arrived at this startling conclusion after lecturing and practicing the dynamics of leadership in business for many years. He also announced that this opinion was not so much based on a faith conviction but rather on scientific data that measures effective leadership in the modern world. Ken Blanchard and Phil Hodges, co-authors of the *One Minute Manager*, and more than forty other books, founded the "Lead Like Jesus" movement based somewhat on the Greenleaf model but greatly enhanced with the integration of Sacred Scripture.

Eventually a Catholic version of "Leading Like Jesus" arrived on the leadership horizon under the inspiration of Owen Phelps in collaboration with Blanchard. Dr. Phelps, writer, college professor, and consultant to the Communications Committee of the U.S. Catholic Conference of Catholic Bishops, founded the Yeshiva Catholic International Leadership Institute in Durand, Illinois. He designated the program as "The Catholic Vision for Leading like Jesus—Servant, Steward and Shepherd." I took, and later taught this program, and I definitely recommend it for deacons and church leaders.

Although Catholics are not accustomed to refer to Christ as a servant-leader in our prayers, liturgy, or preaching, I think, upon reflection, we actually view Him as exactly that. It is true Christ is often described as the suffering servant. Why would we be surprised then to hear that what Christ preached, practiced, and taught the people and His disciples twenty centuries ago is being proclaimed today by secular and religious authorities alike as the most effective leadership philosophy.

Most Church authorities of all denominations recognize there is a definite leadership challenge for both laity and clergy. Over the last fifty years the Catholic Church in America has dramatically changed from an immigrant working-class population to one that is among the most highly educated, and one which enjoys sizeable incomes. Catholics excel as leaders in government, business, academia and other professions. Their distinct challenge now is to merge their leadership expertise with the concept of servanthood in their homes, parishes, workplaces, and society. For deacons the challenge is even greater. They are called on to be servant-leaders in their parishes and when they can assume a similar role in their workplaces they can extend their spiritual influence without violating their employer's policies. Deacons can become "profitable servants" for Christ as well as advancing the profit objectives of their companies.

Let me cite several examples from the business world where elements of servant-leadership are practiced for profit and altruism. I taught the Dale Carnegie course for a number of years. Critics claimed some of these programs were based on a philosophy of manipulation. Not true! Dale Carnegie was the son of a Methodist minister. He freely admitted his programs were based on biblical themes. The main theme running through the program was "Do unto others as you would have them do unto you." I witnessed hundreds of attendees change their business and personal lives because they learned how to serve the needs of others. They became leaders because they motivated others to act. I have adopted these principles in my day-to-day ministry.

The joy of helping people in business and in ministry was remarkably rewarding. Many deacons are still working in business and professions. They use their talents to help make their firms profitable. In the diaconate they become highly successful servants for the Lord. The deacon as servant-leader identifies the needs of parishioners and strives to serve those needs. Due to his positive influence, they listen and then follow his example. He brings comfort and joy to them and in turn experiences joy himself.

Another business strategy whose principles may be distinctly related to deacon servanthood I call, "Sincerely Care about Helping People." As vice-president of claims administration for the second largest company in the nation, I was given the challenge to reverse our poor litigation and complaint record. I immediately assigned staff across the country to research literature on customer relations, to attend seminars, interview insurance and state department personnel, and finally, produce a strategy to improve the company's poor image.

It took us a year to develop and implement a program that reversed our negative record. I asked our staff to reduce the total endeavor into one descriptive sentence which then became our national marketing motto: "Sincerely Care about Helping People." The program cost the company many millions, but morale soared, we were happier in our jobs, our clients were very grateful and our agents experienced increased sales. Sincerely caring about helping all people is the essence of servanthood in ministry and in business.

A Major Source of Joy

> *"The only ones among you who will be really happy are those who have sought and found how to serve."*   Albert Schweitzer, Nobel Prize Winner, 1952

The practice of Servant-Leadership was practiced by individuals world-wide long before it became an institutionalized management philosophy. One such individual was Dr. Albert Schweitzer (1875-1965). He was a German and later French citizen, theologian, philosopher, physician, and missionary in Lambarene, South Africa. He was also a deacon in the Episcopal Church. Dr. Schweitzer gave up his careers in Germany and France and started a hospital in an old chicken house in South Africa where he and his wife treated the sick. He wrote that despite his numerous accomplishments he experienced real joy as a servant to the poor. There were many others who were extremely successful in their professions who ultimately discovered that the "ultimate secret of joy" was abandoning their fame and fortunes and becoming servants to others.

Beware the "Super Servant" Syndrome

> *"Whatever you do, do it wholeheartedly, out of reverence for the Lord and not for others, knowing that you will receive from the Lord an inheritance; be servants of the Lord Jesus Christ."*   Col 3:23-24

I have observed, over the years, that I, and many of my fellow deacons as well as others involved in ministry, periodically fall into the over-extension trap. "Don't let your branches extend further than your roots grow deep" applies to most people in ministry. We are prone to please everyone and therein lies the perilous pitfall of burnout and loss of joy in service. The question always to be asked, "Am I doing this for God or for myself?" I recall one of the sayings of Mother Teresa, "We will be judged on how much we have loved not on how much we have done."

We may misinterpret St. Paul's most often quoted verse in Philippians 4:13, "I can do all things in Jesus Christ who strengthens me." The exegetical experts clarify the confusion by stating God will give us the power to perform those deeds that are in conformity with His will but in no way does this interpretation preclude the power of God to become the instrument in performing seemingly impossible things, including the miraculous.

Humility—The Essence of Servant Leadership

"Humble leaders don't think less of themselves, they think of themselves less."   Ken Blanchard

Humility is the *"sine qua non"* of authentic servant leadership. The deacon is urged to die to himself daily if he truly desires to be a servant and leader in his church community. I recall a conversation with fellow deacons during which a colleague suddenly confided in us, "Hey guys, I finally got humility." We thought he was joking....he was deadly serious. It was difficult for us to mask our amusement. Later when we would meet, one of us would announce, "Gentlemen I've just had my first book published." Going along with the gag, we would ask, "What's the title?" With a grin he would reply, *Humility and How I Achieved It.* Acquiring real humility is a life-long process. If we even think we have achieved it....we haven't.

The Call to a Life of Holiness

"I slept and dreamed life was joy. I awoke and saw that life was service. I acted and behold: Service was joy!"   Rabindranath Tagore

On October 20, 1993, Pope St. John Paul II, at his general audience, described deacon spirituality when he noted that "the special grace conferred through Ordination strengthens the deacon's natural gifts in order to conform him more fully to Jesus Christ." Pope Paul VI in his document, *Sacrum Diaconatus Ordinum* described further the diaconate duties: "Deacons serve the mysteries of Christ and the Church, and must abstain from any vice, strive to please God, and be 'ready for any good work' for the salvation of men. Therefore, because of their reception of the Order, they should far excel others in their liturgical lives, in devotion to prayer in the divine ministry, in obedience, charity, and chastity" (n. 25, *Enchiridion Vaticanum*, II, 1395).

Further, in his document, Pope Paul VI describes the spiritual activities in which deacons should engage:

• Apply themselves to reading carefully and to meditating attentively on the word of God.

• Attend Mass frequently—even daily if possible—receive the Blessed Sacrament of the Eucharist and visit it out of devotion.

• Purify their souls frequently through the sacrament of penance, having prepared for it worthily through a daily examination of conscience.

• Show a deep filial love and veneration for the Virgin Mary, the Mother of God (cf. ibid; n26: *Enchiridion Vaticanum*, II, 1396).

Spirituality vs. Religiosity

Deacons, like other clerics, may eventually become so immersed in the externals of liturgy and religious practices that their performance becomes rote, superficial, and simply "a job." There is a great temptation to focus on the symbols and forget the purpose of ministry which is to "bring people to a closer relationship with Christ." Religion literally means binding oneself to certain dogmas, teachings, rubrics, articles of faith, etc., whereas true spirituality means having a deep and abiding friendship with God.

Deacons who "get into trouble" typically have abandoned or neglected a vigorous prayer life. It begins with failing to pray the Liturgy of the Hours, meditation, daily Mass (when possible) and true involvement with the people of the parish. The lukewarm deacon then falls victim to the worst aspects of clericalism; begins to criticize his pastor, the Bishop, the Church and eventually as a malcontent becomes totally ineffective. He forgets that he was ordained to be a "Servant" and seeks recognition, power, prestige, and privilege of rank.

The Deacon as a Beacon

"Let your light shine upon men that they may see your good works and give glory to your father." Mt 5:16

The nun was asking the third-grade class if they could describe the various ranks of church clerics. When the discussion came to a description of a deacon the pupils became silent. Suddenly Sally shouted, "Sister, I know, a deacon is a man who sits high on a hill all day but at night he waves a big lantern to warn the people on ships from sinking at sea."

It seems to me that Sally was at least half right. Most deacons I know don't have time to sit around all day but are in the business of helping people whether at sea or on land. Deacons have been variously described as icons, leaven, servant-leaders, and bridges between the world and the Church. I would now like to add that they may also be known as beacons of light. I believe deacons would agree these titles are not ones they always deserve but rather roles toward which they might aspire. Deacons should not be defined exclusively by what they do but who they are. I think the deacon as a beacon of spiritual light can more truly reflect the essence of who he is or should be. He is called upon to reflect the light of his soul, his inner being, his spirituality so that those who see it will be greatly influenced and guided by it.

There is no mandated or unique method to achieve holiness, but the substance and core of the deacon's spirituality is his intimate relationship with Christ and desire to love and serve all. He cannot project the light of Christ to others unless he has first acquired it himself. Most Reverend Robert D. Gruss, Bishop of Rapid City, South Dakota, expresses this sentiment well in his article, "A Message for Deacons." "Because of Ordination, deacons are configured to Christ in a special relationship...this relationship must be nurtured each day by the way the deacon enters into a life of prayer beyond the Mass and the sacraments, beyond fulfilling the promise to pray daily the Liturgy of the Hours. He must live in that special relationship that comes from being ordained. The deacon must live in this union through a life of prayer."

Albert Schweitzer once stated: "In everyone's life, at some time, our own light goes out and is rekindled and then bursts into flames by an encounter with another person. Each of us has cause to think with deep gratitude of those who have lighted the flame within us." Many deacons at some time in their life have this experience. Their beacon of light begins to fade. It is my hope as they read some passage in this book, through the power of the Holy Spirit, that spiritual flame will be reignited and they will continue to be a beacon of light to all whom they serve.

The Band of Deacon Brothers—The Fraternal Bond That Binds Us

During the long years of training, deacon candidates develop a close-knit relationship with each other that continues long after they are ordained. Unlike in the military, social organizations or academic institutions, the fraternal bond created is unique among deacons because of the spiritual dynamic that binds them together. In later years the opportunities to connect are limited to annual retreats, conferences as well as Vicariate meetings but the close camaraderie continues. I have often noticed that similar to priests, most deacons have their own brand of humor. It's usually self-deprecating and focused on their foibles or embarrassing events in their ministry. The most significant characteristic they exhibit however, is that special attitude of joy. One thing most deacons do not condone is a prideful attitude or pretentiousness among their brother deacons.

I Never Looked Back

"No one who puts his hand to the plow and then looks back is fit for the kingdom of God."   Lk 9:62

The majority of deacons persevere in their clerical role as long as they are able to serve. In my ordination class of twenty-eight, only one left the diaconate for personal reasons. There are many reasons for the high degree of perseverance. Most are married and are quite mature upon entering this life-time commitment and have a myriad of life experiences. The gift of perseverance, which we are encouraged to constantly pray for, is the most common reason for remaining in the trenches. Mandatory retirement in most dioceses is age seventy-five. Why do we stay and even continue in retirement? Because we love it!! It is a vocation of Joy!

I will soon celebrate my thirty-fifth year in diaconal ministry. The two best decisions I made in my life were to marry my wife Eileen and become a deacon. Like most deacons, my life had its share of sorrows and major disappointments, but the joy I have experienced serving God and my parish community far exceeded the negative events in my life. When I say "I never looked back," I do not express it in a boastful manner but rather as a prayer of gratitude to God for the grace of perseverance. As Scripture says: "The joy of the Lord is your strength" (Neh 8:10).

Chapter 5

THE JOYFUL MINISTER OF LITURGIES

"By virtue of the sacrament received, an indelible spiritual character is impressed, which makes the Deacon, in a permanent and real way, a minister of Christ therefore he is no longer a layman."

Pope John Paul II, November 30, 1995,
Meeting with the Congregation of Clergy.

Holy Orders—The Apostolic Ministries

A deacon is ordained for a life of service. His apostolic ministry is threefold: service of the word, service of the altar, and service of charity. As I previously stated, his role and responsibilities include preaching, teaching, evangelizing, performing baptisms, solemnly witnessing marriages, assisting at Mass, distributing the Holy Eucharist, and conducting wakes and cemetery committals. In addition, he may be involved in many other ministries, such as hospital and prison visitation, counseling, and various assignments by his Bishop or pastor.

The dedicated deacon experiences a special joy in performing these various ministries, because he knows he is exercising the mission of Christ and spiritually affecting untold thousands. Next to assisting the Celebrant at Mass and distributing the Holy Eucharist, I find I derive a special joy in the privilege of preaching. I realize the Holy Spirit speaks through me as the homilist and His word does help people change their lives, renew their faith and hope, and convey consolation for their troubled hearts. This knowledge gives me a special feeling of joy that I can be used, or for that matter needed, to spread the Good News.

Preparing to Preach

"Indeed the word of God is living and effective, sharper than any two-edged sword, penetrating even between soul and spirit, joints and marrow and able to discern reflections and thoughts of the heart."   Heb 4:12

The Scripture verse above, I believe, expresses the first function the deacon must perform in preparing the homily: First, let the "word of God penetrate his soul and spirit" through prayer, reflection, *Lectio Divina*, and the working of the Holy Spirit. Unlike their pastors who frequently preach several Sunday Masses and also daily Mass, the deacons who may only preach several times a month, have the luxury of more time to research, reflect, pray, and produce their homilies. We need to ask the questions, "Am I living the message I intend to convey to the people next Sunday? How is God's word working in my own life?"

Pope Francis, in his encyclical *The Joy of the Gospel*, issues this warning to clergy preparing the homily, "Yet, if he does not take time to hear God's word with an open heart, if he does not let it touch his life, to challenge him, to impress him, and if he does not devote time to pray with that word, then he will indeed be a false prophet, a fraud, a shallow imposter." That's pretty tough but helpful advice.

As a further reminder of the sacred privilege of preaching, we might recall the bishop's mandate at our ordination: "Receive the Gospel of Christ whose herald you now are: Believe what you read, teach what you believe, and practice what you teach!"

Like most deacons, I have collected, over the years, many books and attended many workshops on the art of preaching. Formulating a homily is a serious process but it should also be a joyful one. I struggle in preparing my homilies, but the joy of completing and preaching them is gratifying. Perfecting our preaching is a lifetime process and few of us will ever be an Archbishop Sheen or The Reverend Billy Graham, but we need to strive for constant improvement. God and our congregations deserve only our best.

The Real Joy in Preaching

"We do not proclaim ourselves. Rather we proclaim Jesus Christ as Lord, and ourselves as your servants for the sake of Jesus."   2 Cor 4:5

The deacon homilist approaches the Book, blesses the *Missal*, signs himself and prays, "May the words of the Gospel wipe away our sins." In this prayer of humility he concedes he also is a sinner and this admission creates the proper attitude as he is about to preach. It helps me realize I am simply the implement or mouthpiece of the Holy Spirit, preaching through me. I am only the medium...the message is Christ. The deacon should be reassured by the words of Isaiah 55:14, "So shall my word be that goes forth from my mouth. It should not return to me void, but shall do my will, achieving the end for which I sent it."

For the life of me I cannot squelch a concern, even after thirty-four years of preaching. St. Paul identifies this fear in 1 Corinthians 9:27, "Rather, I discipline my body and bring it under control, for fear that after preaching to others I myself may be disqualified." When I preach to others I realize I may fail to perform what I preach, or worse, fall into the sin I condemn. This sobering thought is an excellent deterrent to pride. Therein lies one of the advantages in preparing the homily. The deacon has a chance to think and meditate about what he intends to say. He compares the message he will share with the congregation with how well he is practicing it in his daily life and prays that he will take that message to heart.

One Sunday, when I was preaching about sin, I commented that I also was a sinner. After Mass a concerned parishioner took me aside and said, "Deacon John, you should never, ever state you are a sinner! We put our clergy on a pedestal of virtue. You lose credibility with the parishioners when you make such a confession." I tried to explain that we all fall short of perfection, but he walked away just shaking his head.

There is more good-natured humor among deacons about their homiletic efforts than any other aspect of their ministries. It arises not out of disrespect, but the admission of our own inadequacies. Poking fun at ourselves and one another keeps us humble. It is also a subtle sign we are enjoying what we do. I'm pretty certain that this has happened to quite a few deacons and even priests: The deacon was greeting parishioners as they left Mass when a lady stopped and remarked, "Deacon Tim, you preached a marvelous homily this morning." The deacon thanked her and was a bit pleased with himself. But she quickly added, "That deacon last Sunday talked for almost a half-hour and said absolutely nothing! You did it in twelve minutes."

Sometimes, it is not what the homilist preaches, but what the congregation hears. This is often pointed out when several congregants approach the homilist after Mass and each relate a different inspirational message they received. The deacon accepts that it was not the point he intended, but rather it was the Holy Spirit working through him. If brevity is the soul of wit it is the second soul of the sermon; the first is adapting the Scripture to the real needs of the hearers. "Be brief, but say much in those few words, be like the wise man, taciturn" (Sir 32:8).

A majority of homiletic experts agree that an effective homily should not exceed ten to twelve minutes. They also claim if you can't make your point in that time, you will muddle the message and lose your audience. I admit I have endeavored for years to stay within those time parameters. My colleagues do tease me but I'm still trying.

One Sunday when my homily exceeded the recommended ten minutes, the visiting priest announced to the congregation, "In the seminary we were told when you see people glancing at their watches, it's a signal to start your conclusion. But when they shake their watches and hold them to their ears you better wind up your homily immediately. I'm sure Deacon John will take the hint." I accepted the lesson. For several weeks after the "issue" some of the ushers good naturedly threatened to shake their watches if I violated the time limit.

The Point and Purpose of the Homily

We are taught to pick out just one verse in the reading and one point that will relate to people's needs and then demonstrate how Christ's word will help them in their daily lives. Linking the Gospel to actual concerns of the people in the pews is hard work. Like most homilists, I find that delving into interpretive texts, praying about the major point or pearl that speaks to me and then sensitively listening to what people are crying out for is spiritually, emotionally, and intellectually rewarding. I love the entire process. I experience a special type of joy. I'm praying and preaching to myself first and hopefully through my efforts the word of God will also touch and change the hearts of the listeners.

Developing a Taste for Sacred Scripture

"Your words are sweet to my palate, even sweeter to my tongue than honey."   Ps 119:103

Biblical scholars tell us that the Hebrew mothers, in order to encourage their young children to love the Torah, would lightly brush honey on some of the pages. At an early age the children would thus connect sweetness with the word of God. The prophet Ezekiel was ordered by God to go even further by actually consuming the scroll. " 'Son of man,' he said to me, 'eat what is set before you...' So I opened my mouth and He gave me the scroll to eat. 'Son of man' he then said, 'feed your belly and fill your stomach with the scroll I am giving to you.' I ate it and it was sweet as honey in my mouth" (Ezek 3:1-3). When we reverence the Gospel and fall in love with the Word we are consumed by it and it becomes part of us. Our hearts speak intimately to the hearts of our hearers.

The Ultimate Joy in the Mass and Eucharist

"Then I will go to the altar of God, to the God of my joy and delight, and I will praise you with the harp, O God, my God."   Ps 43:4

Priests agree that celebrating Mass is the most sacred and rewarding event in their daily lives. Most deacons would also confirm that the privilege of assisting the Celebrant at the altar and participating in the Holy Eucharist is the highlight of our ministry. An unknown author gave deacons this advice, "Assist the celebrant at Mass as though it's your first; as though it's your only Mass; as though it's your last Mass." When I ascend the altar with the Celebrant my mind often flashes back to my altar serving days and the opening prayer: "I will go unto the altar of God, the God who gives joy to my youth." The Holy Eucharist is known as "the source and summit of our faith." It is also the source of our strength in ministry and the core ingredient of our diaconal identity.

We Hold Christ in the Palm of Our Hand

"May God hold you in the palm of His hand." This verse is taken from an ancient Irish prayer and is one of my favorites. When I recite it I am reminded that we, in turn, hold Christ in the palm of our hand. What an awesome reality to know that we, as ministers of the Eucharist, literally, not symbolically, hold Christ in our hands as we share Him with the communicants. How much more reverence we would show if we would focus on this remarkable privilege.

I recently had the opportunity to see my two-week old grandson for the first time. What a joyful experience to cuddle this seven-pound red-headed infant in my arms as I marveled at the miracle of his birth. There are fewer events in this world that exceed the deep joy that family members experience in caressing and loving a tiny infant. In handing back this small bundle of joy to his mother, my daughter, I did so carefully, tenderly, and thankful for the privilege. Later, when distributing Holy Communion at Mass, I recalled that emotional moment...I held a little child and then gave him to his mother. How much greater was the privilege and honor to now hold Christ in my hand and to give Him to others.

We might recall the experience of Simeon at the Presentation of the Child Jesus in the Temple. "He took him in his arms and praised God saying, 'Now, Lord, you may dismiss your servant in peace, according to your word; for my eyes have seen your salvation, which you have prepared in the sight of all the peoples, a light of revelation to the Gentiles and glory for your people Israel'" (Lk 2:28). Simeon held Jesus only once, while we, as ministers of the Eucharist, have the exquisite privilege of holding Him thousands upon thousands of times and then sharing the Body of Christ with communicants.

Unfortunately, we have witnessed how some celebrants, deacons, and ministers of the Eucharist distribute Holy Communion as though they were passing out tickets at a ball game or distributing programs to concert goers. In contrast, we are so edified when observing the minister hold the Sacred Host aloft, slowly say, "The Body of Christ," look the communicant in the eye, and gently place the Holy Eucharist in the palm or on their tongue. Parishioners notice how we reverence the Eucharist and generally will respond in kind. This is not the time to rush, but it is a precious opportunity to experience the joy of receiving, holding, and sharing Christ. We are indeed Christ-bearers.

One of the dangers the deacon constantly faces in celebrating the various liturgies is falling into the rut of routine. Repetition can breed perfunctory performance. Deacon Kevin Bagley describes attitude as a lack of intentionality. In his excellent article, "Rubrics, Just the Beginning,"(*Deacon Digest*, July, 2014) he writes, "Are we intentional when we perform a series of motions, movements, and tasks to accomplish our sacramental action, or are they just movements to accomplish a task? We have been graced with the charism of the diaconate by our ordination and we bring Christ into our actions and encounters so that those to whom we minister can enter more deeply into the mysteries we share."

The Sacraments

After many years of diaconal service I am still awestruck when I assist at the altar, witness marriages, perform baptisms, and conduct wake and funeral services. I think about the little lad from the small town in Pennsylvania who was probably the most unlikely candidate for the diaconate. That opinion is not false modesty. "Why have you been so generous to me, O God?", I pray. All this and heaven too! What a joy to participate as a servant in such wondrous things in His name.

Thus far in this book I have spoken almost exclusively about the joy of the diaconate. But we all experience the suffering side of life as well as the joy. In Chapter 6, I will share the aspects of pain and suffering that deacons are exposed to in their multiple ministries.

Matrimony

All priests and deacons, after years in service, will have accumulated an abundance of stories experienced in their ministry. Many are joyful, some quite humorous and others very sad. I once conducted the usual required prenuptial sessions with a couple in their forties. They took the oath to give true answers to all the questions. Our pastor would celebrate the Mass, and I would witness the marriage vows.

Ten minutes before we were scheduled to start, the groom approached me in a panic. "Deacon, I have a confession to make. I have a wife in Europe. Does that really make a difference?" The pastor had to make the announcement to the packed church that the wedding ceremony was cancelled. There was no joy in the church that morning. Married deacons have a distinct advantage in preparing couples for marriage particularly if the deacon's hair has turned silver. The deacon has a lot of credibility in their eyes because he has lived the joys and turmoil of "wedded bliss." Baptisms and weddings are happy occasions, and since deacons are an integral part of the preparation and the ceremony, we get to share vicariously in their joy.

Baptism

Welcoming infants into the Church and the community of faith is not only a time of celebration but an ideal time for evangelizing. Some of the attendees at weddings and baptisms may be non-Catholics or non-practicing Catholics. The deacon, in the brief homily, can demonstrate that ours is a religion of joyfulness and hope. Gathering the family and friends around the baptismal font and making the sacrament an intimate event can leave the attendees with a lasting positive impression. Every deacon will tell you how often peo-

ple will come to them and say what a beautiful ceremony it was to be part of. Those comments alone bring
joy and satisfaction.

Surprisingly, one proof of their appreciation of their
involvement is their reluctance to leave the church
after the baptism. I usually need to wait as they continue their chatting. When I begin turning out the lights,
they get the hint that it's time to leave. It's these small
gestures of caring that reinforce the servant role of a
deacon.

Evangelizing in the Cemetery

Are you kidding? How can the deacon or priest
attempt to evangelize or re-evangelize in a cemetery? I
have discovered, as have many others, that the
Committal Service in the cemetery can present one of
the best opportunities for sowing or re-sowing the seeds
of faith, especially belief in one's personal resurrection
and life after death. I'm not referring to the permanent
residents of course, but to the visitors. Of course, the
cemetery service is the culmination of the process. It
begins at the wake service and continues at the Mass.
We thus have three distinct opportunities to re-evangelize. We know that many of the Catholics at each event
are not practicing their faith or receiving the Sacraments
on a regular basis. I therefore use the 60/40 rule. Forty
percent are probably non-practicing Catholics or members of other Christian denominations.

The bereaved family and friends of the deceased are at their most vulnerable at the time of the death of a beloved. They are crying out for consolation, words of comfort, and some type of spiritual answers...at least many of them are. That's our responsibility as clergy. "He has sent me to bring glad tidings to the lonely, to heal the brokenhearted" (Isa 61:1).

The process begins at the wake service. Before I conduct the formal service, I usually ask the funeral director to invite members of the immediate family to meet with me in a private room for ten minutes or so where I offer my condolences, review the liturgy for the Mass of Resurrection, if one is scheduled, and then discuss the eulogy if one is to be given at the wake, before or after the Mass or at the cemetery. Finally, but most importantly, I spend a few minutes discussing our Christian belief in the Resurrection and eternal life and how that relates not only to the deceased loved one, but to the family as well. We conclude with a brief prayer. The stage is then set for reinforcement of this message of hope at the wake service, the homily at Mass, and then at the cemetery.

Over the years, I have found the two most powerful Scripture passages for both the Gospel proclamation and the homily are John 11:25: "I am the resurrection and the life. Whoever believes in me, even though he dies, will live, and everyone who lives and believes in me will never die." The second verse is from John 14:2: "In my Father's house there are many dwelling places."

Funeral services today are reduced from those of former years. The two-day wake is history. Some opt for a one-evening wake, no Mass, and then cremation. Cremations in the U.S. have tripled since 1985, accounting for about 44 percent of all body disposals. The Cremation Association of North America predicts that figure will rise to 55 percent by 2025. People elect cremation for economic reasons. Others may choose cremation to follow the intent of disguising the reality of death. In those cases where the family desires an abbreviated funeral liturgy, I think it is incumbent on the priest or deacon to provide an especially inspiring service in the brief time available. The family and attendees are most vulnerable since they are reminded of their own mortality. They are more receptive to the message of hope and will welcome Christ's promise of their own personal resurrection.

Chapter 6

JOY IN SUFFERING – THE APPARENT CONTRADICTION

"My brethren, consider it is a cause of great joy whenever you endure various trials, for you know that the testing of your faith will develop perseverance."   Jas 1:2-4

Are joy and suffering compatible? Can one experience both at the same time? Upon first reading the above exhortation of St. James, one would wonder how we can experience joy, and pure joy at that, when we encounter "trials of many kinds."

Thus far in this book I have discussed the multiple sources of joy for deacons, those in ministry, as well as all believers. It's appropriate now to talk about the suffering and sorrows that we experience ourselves and in the lives of those we serve; and then how we can attempt to reconcile joy with suffering.

Deacons are frequently asked by parishioners, who themselves are suffering, or whose family members or friends are in pain, that age-old question, "If God is omnipotent and benevolent why does He cause suffer-

ing and why does He permit pain?" I have great difficulty believing God causes suffering, but He may permit it. In some cases we can clearly see how the abuse
of free will can cause pain and suffering to innocent
victims. In the case of natural disasters that result in
the loss of lives and property, we are left without expla-
nations.

Theologians, spiritual writers, and mystics have
struggled with this imponderable question since the
beginning of time. I have summarized the six different
approaches, supported by many theologians, identified by Fr. Richard Sparks, C.S.P, a contributing
author to *The New Dictionary of Catholic Spirituality*
in attempting to explain the causes or reasons for
human suffering:

- *Dualism*: Where the forces of light are locked in a
  constant worldly battle with the forces of dark-
  ness.
- *Freewill Theodicy*: Mankind causes sin resulting
  in consequential suffering.
- *Retribution and Punishment*: God causes retribution for man's sins through disease, weather
  calamities, and natural disasters.
- *Redemptive Suffering or Atonement*: The guilt-
  less or innocent accept suffering on behalf of others for their sins; the "Suffering Christ" is the best
  example of this.
- *Irenaean Approach*: An incomplete world is still
  in the process of development and its continuing

growth causes natural disasters and suffering. A variant of this theory is that one must suffer through self-imposed mortification, penance, and pain in order to come closer to God.

- *The Faith Solution*: This is the Old Testament Job paradigm in which we simply accept suffering, innocent though we may be, as a mystery. We can only say: "The Lord gave and the Lord has taken away," and surrender to God's will.

We still grapple with the question: "How can we experience joy and suffering at the same time?" The Christian response is based on the model of Christ beginning with His agony in the Garden of Olives and continuing on to His crucifixion. He accepts His suffering and death by trusting in God the Father when He prays, "Father, if you are willing take this cup from me. Yet not my will but yours be done" (Lk 22:42).

Author Shirwood Wirt, in his book, *Jesus Man of Joy,* asks the question: "Where does joy come in all this suffering?" He then responds: "The answer in the Bible is that faith itself creates joy. Faith leads to contentment, and contentment leads to peace, and peace brings into play all the other fruits of the Spirit, including love and joy.

What Should the Deacon Do?

"What does the Church need most at this historic moment? I see clearly that the thing the Church needs most today is the ability to heal wounds and to warm the hearts of the faithful; it needs nearness, proximity. I see the Church as a field hospital after battle....And you dear brothers—I ask you—do you know the wounds of your parishioners? Do you perceive them? Are you close to them? It's the only question" (*Address of Pope Francis to Parish Priests of the Diocese of Rome, March 6, 2014*).

Deacons also need to hear and respond to the "wounds" of the people as Pope Francis urges in the above citation. We used to use the phrase, "Offer it up (to Christ)" when attempting to console people in pain. Over the years clergy and others who walk with those who are suffering attempt to be more helpful and compassionate. Deacons are obligated, through the mercy they receive from God, to extend His mercy to them. Author Jon Sobrino writes, "Mercy is a basic attitude toward the suffering of another, whereby one reacts to eradicate that suffering for the sole reason that it exists." Julia Upton, in "Mercy," in *The Dictionary of Spirituality* adds, "Mercy is the compassionate care of others whereby one takes on the burden of another as one's own." And our merciful Pope Francis in his Angelus message on April 6, 2014 unequivocally states, "Listen carefully: there is no limit to the divine mercy offered to everyone!"

I find that in addition to praying with a person, actively listening to them and just being present with them goes a long way in comforting them. In this life we may never know or understand the reason for unexplained personal suffering. When after talking and praying with someone who continues to experience emotional or physical pain, I find the following approach helpful:

- Continue contact and communication with the suffering client.
- Be present to them in a personal and non-authoritative way.
- Remind them we will not forget or abandon them.
- Pray openly with them; use Sacred Scripture frequently. Some biblical passages that may give them comfort are these: "I consider that the sufferings we presently endure are not worth comparing with the glory to be revealed in us"(Rom 8:18); "Eye has not seen, ear has not heard, nor has the human heart imagined what God has prepared for those who love him" (1Cor 2:9); "Be brave and steadfast; have no fear or dread of them, for it is the Lord, your God, who marches with you; He will never fail or forsake you" (Deut 31:6); "We know God makes all things work together for good for those who love him and who are called according to his purpose" (Rom 8:28). This latter verse means we should trust totally in His wisdom and the reason for our suffering. It also means we can have the abiding conviction that we will live forever in eternal joy where there will be no tears or suffering.

- Urge them, despite their pain, to reach out every day and help another suffering person.
- Focus on Christ as their companion in suffering; in relating to His passion they will find solace of soul.
- Urge frequent reception of the Holy Eucharist. This is not only the "Source and Summit" of our faith but the most powerful source of grace and spiritual strength one can ever experience.

I remember a certain situation in which I exhausted most of the foregoing approaches with a middle-aged man who was a chronic alcoholic. I was conducting a "family intervention" during which the family members read aloud their letters in which they shared how his addiction was causing them and his grandchildren a lot of pain and anxiety. His pain and self-loathing was intense. He finally agreed to enter a rehabilitation facility that I had arranged. At the last moment he advised us that he had changed his mind. I heard nothing from him for several months until one day he approached me with a huge smile and hug. "Deacon John, I just returned from rehab. I'm in recovery and back with my family. I can't tell you how happy we are." Prayer always works but in God's good time.

In attempting to console and counsel suffering people I find that they often experience a measure of comfort and joy but it may come later. Those who minister to the emotional and physical needs of those in pain will also receive a certain measure of joy. As a deacon, I always feel a deep sense of peace and joy in praying with and offering comfort to the sick and suffering. It can be a win-win spiritual outcome for both.

What Are the Benefits of Suffering?

Physicians tell us that physical pain and suffering generally are a signal that there is an underlying physical problem. We should be grateful for that warning and the opportunity to do something about it. When it comes to giving definitive answers to the spiritual benefits of suffering, I'll leave the more comprehensive answer to that question to the theologians. We do know through Christ's suffering and death we gained redemption and life everlasting. In the lives of the saints there are dramatic examples of how their suffering caused their conversion. St. Ignatius Loyola suffered a wound in battle and during his extensive rehabilitation he changed his whole lifestyle and eventually founded the Society of Jesus.

Our own pain and suffering can motivate us to become more compassionate to others and submissive to God's will. It can also generate anger, resentment, and despair. I prefer love and joy as a greater catalyst for conversion, but take notice to what theologian, Father Ron Rolheiser writes in his book *Holy Longing*:

"Any good psychologist, spiritual director, or mentor of souls, will tell you that, most often, real growth and maturity of soul are triggered by deep suffering and pain in our lives. It's not so much that

God doesn't speak as clearly to us in our joys and successes, but we tend not to be listening in those moments. Suffering gets our attention. As C.S. Lewis once said, pain is God's microphone to a deaf world. There is, undeniably, a connection between suffering and depth of soul."

I bow to Reverend Rolheiser's theological wisdom as well as those "psychologists, spiritual directors, and mentors of souls," but I believe to give love and to receive love with an open heart, is still the most powerful motivator in the world for change. I felt relieved when Rolheiser later wrote, "But we must be careful not to read too much into this. When we look at Jesus, and many other wonderfully healthy people, we see that depth of soul is also connected to the joyous and celebratory moments in life."

Last year I was scheduled for a pre-surgical interview with the head surgeon at the New York Hospital for Special Surgery. Three orthopedic surgeons confirmed that five herniated discs were the primary cause of the severe back pain that was making my life miserable and my ministry difficult. I prayed every day for relief. At the same time, I was writing a book on trusting God in all things based on my favorite verse, St. Paul's letter to the Romans 8:28: "And we know God makes all things work together for good for those who love him and are called according to his purpose." The debilitating pain gradually subsided.

Despite the strong urging of the orthopedists that I undergo surgery, I cancelled the operation. I relied on the power of prayer and used the "Faith Approach." A minor miracle? I don't know, but I'm certain that if God permits suffering to occur He also will hear our prayers and sometimes even remove our suffering. Was I able to maintain my inner joy while enduring persistent pain? Yes, to a much greater degree than what I could achieve in similar circumstances years ago. I applied to my own situation the approaches to handling suffering that I had been preaching to others. The physician began to heal himself through the grace of God.

Jesus the Man of Sorrows

"He was spurned and avoided by men, a man of suffering, accustomed to infirmity."   *Isa 53:3*

For centuries, the Church put much emphasis in its teachings, preaching, and liturgy on the passion and death of Christ, sin, and mortification. In poetry, paintings, and sculpture Christ was more often configured as a suffering savior with a stern and solemn appearance. It's only in the last few decades that we have seen a more pronounced attempt to also portray Christ as joyful.

The entire chapter of Isaiah 53 is one of the most descriptive of Christ's future suffering and death but the bulk of the Scripture readings proclaim "good tidings" in all circumstances. Sherwood E. Wirt, in his joyful book *Jesus, Man of Joy*, gives an excellent clarification of Isaiah's passage 55:3 "Jesus, the man of sorrows acquainted with grief." Wirt writes, "When Christian writers describe Christ as a "man of sorrow," they are not describing His inner nature. Jesus' grief was sometimes a result of flogging and curses; sorrow came entirely from without but the joy remained within. "If Jesus became acquainted with grief, it was only to endure it."

The Reality and Longevity of Temptations—A Different Type of Suffering

"God is faithful and he will not allow you be tried beyond your strength but together with the trial he will also provide a way out and the strength to bear it."
                                                      1 Cor 10:13

Deacons are subject to the same temptations that affect lay people and perhaps more so. Like priests and religious, they are a special target of Satan "who goes about the world seeking whom he may devour." These temptations run the whole gamut but probably the greatest is the temptation of pride. Parishioners tend to put the clergy on a pedestal...and sometimes deacons are inclined to believe they deserve it.

Because deacons are not immune to temptation, it gives them a greater degree of compassion and understanding of how others struggle with their demons. In our counseling and preaching we can give advice and encouragement to their urgent needs. There is power in 2 Corinthians 12:9, "My grace is sufficient for you, for power is made perfect in weakness."

Once when a parishioner queried a deacon about the best way to avoid temptation, the young deacon responded, "Don't worry about that, as you grow older it will avoid you." That advice is not always true, as many of us know. St. Augustine, when asked a similar question, replied, "Temptations finally cease three days after you're dead."

When I was giving a lecture to deacon candidates, I mentioned that the grace of ordination gives them a special strength in their ministry, but your alb, stole, and dalmatic are not made of Teflon. Your vestments do not insulate you from temptations. You are still human. One of the candidates later pulled me aside, and I could see he was visibly upset. He genuinely believed once ordained he would be free of the temptation to sin. I'm sure he has learned differently by now.

Priests are bound by celibacy at the time of their ordination. Deacons are also bound should their wives predecease them; they cannot remarry. Some question this rule, but most deacons I know are not concerned. Dispensations are rare, and if granted, then the deacon is laicized. My wife was once questioned by a parishioner about the remarriage rule, "Can John marry again should you die, God forbid?" "Even if he could, who would have him?" she retorted with a sly grin.

That Your Joy Might Be Complete

"I have told you these things so that my joy may be in you and your joy may be complete. This is My commandment, love one another as I have loved you."   Jn 15:11-12

The world is crying out for genuine love and joy. We all crave the real thing but often seek it in the wrong places. We yearn for love that will endure and joy that will last. We have one of the answers to this yearning for love and joy in Christ's command in John 14:23-24: "Love one another as I have loved you." One of the most difficult challenges Christians face every day of our lives is to obey that exhortation of Christ. Deacons are no exception in not heeding this command. In ministry we do meet people who sometimes do not cooperate in helping solve their own problems despite our assistance. We are human and become exasperated. We fail, falter, and rise again realizing this is our ministry to love all despite their weaknesses. When we do love unconditionally I believe Christ's promise of "complete joy" as a reward is one of the most pronounced assurances of Christ in the Gospel.

What then do we mean by love? That question ranks right up there with the proverbial question, "What is truth?" We use the word so loosely it can lose its original meaning. We use it to describe our affection for both animate and inanimate objects without distinction. For example, "I love my new Lexus automobile, I love the Yankees baseball team, I really love spaghetti and meatballs, etc." What we really mean is that we like those objects. Theologians and philosophers still have difficulty in attempting to define the different types of love. There seems to be general agreement among the majority that there are four major types of love. The first is called conjugal love which exists between the husband and wife who pledge to lifetime fidelity and total giving of themselves. Pope Francis at a General Audience at St. Peter's Square in Rome, in discussing the current negative issues impacting marriages, stated, "The love between a man and woman is God's Masterpiece."

There are probably more jokes and humorous stories related about marriage than any other topic. Despite the problems that arise and must be overcome in the typical marriage, the relationship can and does generate a special type of joy for married people. And therein lies another source of joy for those deacons who are married. They receive both matrimonial sacramental grace and the special joy of spousal intimacy and blessing of family life. When I mentioned to a fellow deacon how blessed we were to receive the Sacraments of Matrimony as well as Holy Orders, he exclaimed, "Wow! All this and heaven, too."

The second type of love called *storge*, is that love of parents for their children and that shown among sisters and brothers. The third category, more familiar to us, is known as *philia*, and the type of love Christ urges us to show to everyone—friends, strangers, and enemies alike. *Agape*, the fourth type of love is the one God shows for all of us. It is the noblest, most compassionate and self-sacrificing. *Philia* and *agape* are the most frequently mentioned in Sacred Scripture. In fact the word love appears 348 times. I don't think Christ made any theological distinctions when He commanded us to love one another. He asked us to love all unconditionally, and when we do our joy will be complete.

Who the Deacon is Not

"This above all, to thine own self be true, and it must follow, as the night the day, thou canst not then be false to any man."

—*William Shakespeare, Hamlet, Act 1, Scene 3*

You might wonder why I follow up the section on suffering and joy with a discussion on the deacon's true identity and legitimate role. I think they are both connected. When we are not true to ourselves and attempt to go beyond our designated diaconal role we are cheating ourselves and dishonest with others. We deprive ourselves of the inner joy and sometimes cause pain to others.

Deacons are not priests nor should they ever pose or pretend they are priests. It would seem unnecessary even to mention this but unfortunately there have been instances where a few deacons become confused about their proper diaconal roles. There exists a significant distinction between the priest and deacon. Priests and deacons should form a perfect ministerial pair. The deacon functions complement those of the priest and occasionally it's the wise deacon who also compliments his pastor.

The Trouble with Father

Every deacon has been incorrectly addressed as "Father" many times, especially when he is in his early years of diaconate. In my first years after ordination, when parishioners would call me "Father," I would take great pains to explain, "I'm not a priest, only a deacon." It initially was a bit awkward but later I found using a little humor was the best solution. I would often reply, "Yes, I am a father of five and a grandfather of fifteen." Once a woman came up to me after Mass and gushed, "Father, that was a home-run sermon you just gave." I simply smiled and thanked her. It was a visiting priest, twenty years my junior, who delivered the excellent homily. Who said deacons don't enjoy humorous moments in ministry!

Then there was the distinguished gentleman who approached the deacon after Mass and commented, "Deacon Ralph, you gave such an inspiring homily, you always do. You know, you should have your homilies published." "No time for that now, but perhaps posthumously," replied the deacon. "Well then, the sooner the better," the gentleman responded.

Of course there are times when the deacon has to remind himself that humility is the best response. I have had occasions, when assigned to do a Baptism, I called the couple and identified myself as a deacon and the response was, "No thanks, we would prefer a real priest." On a few occasions when I was assigned a wedding the mother-of-the-bride stated emphatically, "No offense, deacon, but my daughter really wants an ordained priest." The response on these occasions would vary but it would amount to, "I understand, I'll see what I can do, but if Father is not available you will have to put up with me." Sometimes a spoonful of sugar and a tad of humility may change their minds. Humor can preserve our joy and eliminate any pain or resentment.

Who You Are as a Deacon

"A deacon's worth is not what he is or what he does but because of who he is."

Monsignor James P. McManimon

Some people define their identity with what they do, their job or profession, rather than who they are. Probably one of the best descriptions of who a deacon really is was written by a priest whom I greatly admired and who was very instrumental in counseling me in the early years of my diaconate preparation. The following description of "Who a Deacon Is" was delivered by Monsignor James P. McManimon to a group of deacons

and deacon candidates in 1979. Monsignor McMani-
mon was the founding father and first Director of the
Office of Diaconate in the Diocese of Trenton, New
Jersey.

"It doesn't matter that you are the only deacon in the
parish, or the longest ordained deacon, or the smartest
or most popular, the pastor's confidant. It is of little
consequence that you are from one of the stalwart or
oldest families in the parish, a friend of the Bishop, or
that you are past Grand Knight or former president of
the parish Holy Name Society, or once was the president of the Parish Council.

"Nor does it matter that you are quite adept at
preaching, always preaching, always present at every
weekend Mass, do all the baptismal preparations, do all
the wake services and assist at every funeral, that you
teach religious education and do the Confirmation
retreat every year, that you schedule and train the
Eucharistic ministers, altar servers and lectors, and visit
every hospital within 20 miles of the parish church and
are on-call for opening up the church when it snows.

"What matters is who you are. What is your relationship with God? Are you a person of prayer? Are
you and your wife a manifestation of God's love to one
another, to your children, to the world? In the end,
these are the things that matter; these are the elements
that define who you are as a person, that make you
what you are as a deacon."

Chapter 7

PARTNERS WITH GOD

"We know that God makes all things work together for good for those who love him and who are called according to his purpose."
Rom 8:28

I experience tremendous assurance and consolation when I reflect on St. Paul's passage above. It conveys a special feeling of joy and serenity in knowing, despite life's problems, all things that happen will ultimately "work together for good," when I follow His will. I cite this verse frequently when comforting grieving parishioners, the seriously ill, spouses in troubled marriages, and those suffering from addictions.

When St. Paul writes, "We know," he uses the Greek word *oidamen* which is more powerful and goes beyond the usual "we think," or "we hope." There is no speculation when he makes this statement. The word connotes absolute knowledge beyond all doubt that God will definitely deliver on His promise and it is God working together with us. "All things" includes everything but sin. God permits sin and evil to occur but He does not create it. Man's sinful use of his free will and the influence of Satan are responsible for much of the brokenness in life.

Some biblical interpreters explain "working together" as God, in His providential way, causes all things to work together, but do not mention that God may be using people to assist in His work. Other scholars suggest that God works with us and we with Him. We become both partners with God and beneficiaries. Sometimes, because of pride, we feel we can work things out without God's assistance or guidance. Perhaps the following story might illustrate the folly of the "working alone syndrome."

At their Annual Conference a team of scientists announced their research could now duplicate or even exceed the marvels of God's creation. They sent a delegation to God advising that He had become an anachronism and was no longer relevant in this modern day of scientific discoveries. "We can now replicate or clone all parts of a human being," they boasted. God mused a bit at this prideful claim and responded, "I hear you but why don't we test your discovery and have a creation contest?" "We welcome the challenge!" they eagerly replied.

"Very well," God smiled. "Let's go back to Paradise and begin with the creation of Adam."

"Excellent idea," the scientists shouted and began to scoop up several handfuls of earth to begin their creation effort. "Hold on there! "God interrupted. "You must first go and get your own dirt."

The word "good" in Paul's verse may be interpreted as our spiritual and physical welfare, or eternal salvation, or our closer proximity with God. Evidence of this good may not always be experienced during our lifetime and this may tempt some to think God does not keep His promises. We cannot define "good" as only what we taste, touch, feel, and see during our present existence. Much of Paul's passage deals with our present suffering. Paul clarifies it in Romans 8:18, "For I consider that our present sufferings cannot even be compared to the glory that will be revealed to us." This final "good" is that we at last will inherit eternal life, see the face of God, and experience unspeakable joy forever. Our anticipation of the delivery of this promise gives us an intense feeling of joy even now.

"Called according to his purpose," is the other side of the coin. To be called is to be invited to participate in His plan or purpose for us now and in eternity. Early in the Old Testament the prophet Jeremiah (29:11) has God speaking about His plans for us: "For I know well the plans I have in mind, says the Lord, plans for your welfare, not for woe, plans to give you a future of hope."

A Summary of the Sources of Our Joy

I have described, thus far, many of the sources of joy that deacons may experience in their ministerial activities. Their main source of joy, of course, is their intimate relationship with God. All other origins stem from that relationship. Following is a summary and reminder of the many ways deacons can derive joy in their diaconate vocation:

- Ordained as a Permanent Deacon—He receives the special grace of the Sacrament of Holy Orders.
- Ascends the Altar of God—He assists the Celebrant in the Sacrifice of the Mass and receives Christ into the tabernacle of his soul.
- Dispenses Sacraments—He baptizes and solemnly witnesses marriages.
- Proclaims the Gospel and Preaches the Word of God—He becomes a conduit of the Holy Spirit as he spiritually nourishes and is nourished by communicating the Good News in homilies and the Gospel.
- Ministry of Charity—He is involved in multiple ministries utilizing his various talents.
- Servant-Leader—He is a servant to all and also a leader of others to Christ.
- Spirituality—He is committed to a deep relationship with Christ by virtue of his role as a deacon.
- A Man of Constant Prayer—His life becomes a continuous conversation with God.
- Indwelling of the Holy Trinity—He is aware that the Father, Son and Holy Spirit have taken up residence in his heart.
- Sacred Scripture—He is nourished through biblical reading especially the daily Liturgy of the Hours.

- Stewardship—He dedicates his time, talent, and treasure to God through others.
- Anticipation of Eternal Life—He asks himself: "What is this life compared to eternity?" and has absolute certainty in Christ's promise: "I am the resurrection and the life, whoever believes in me, even though he dies, will live, and everyone who lives and believes in me will never die" (Jn 11:25).

His Word is His Bond

Deacons are gifted with multiple opportunities to bring a message of hope and joy to others in times of sickness, sorrow and death. In addition to reciting the appropriate Scripture, deacons will often use relevant stories to help parishioners understand more fully how Christ's promises bring comfort, hope and even joy at those critical times of their lives.

At the time of the death of a family member or relative the bereaved are crying out for comfort and reassurance that their loved one's faith and belief in their personal resurrection is well founded. Despite their grief they will experience a sense of joy when the deacon reassures them with Christ's promise.

At wakes and cemetery committal services I will frequently share the following personal story to reinforce Christ's promise of eternal life.

I dreaded that inevitable day in August when my dad would summon me and my two brothers with this announcement, "Come on boys we're taking a trip up the mountain to Haycock's coal Tipple. It's time to buy the winter's supply of coal. We lived in a small city nestled in South Central Pennsylvania where coal was cheap and plentiful.

Dad would haggle endlessly with Haycock over the different types of the black stuff. Eventually they would shake hands to seal the agreement. The deal was done. No credit card, check or invoice...three tons of coal for fifteen dollars cash. Delivery guaranteed three months later.

"Dad," I inquired, looking up at his huge hulk as we trudged back down the mountain, "you gave that man fifteen dollars (a sizable sum in those days) and you got nothing in return. How do you know he will even deliver the coal he promised you?" This was one of my earliest moments of distrust in the promises of others.

Dad's reply remains with me still "Son," he said, "That man's word is his bond. I always trust him!" I recall I didn't have a clue what the word "bond" meant but presumed the deal was rock solid since dad did not easily part with a dollar.

Sure enough, one Saturday in October a big truck pulled up to our house and dumped the three tons of shiny black coal on our sidewalk. Mr. Haycock had delivered on his handshake promise. Uncle Ed, some cousins, my dad, my brothers and I shoveled the coal through the front porch windows and into the coal cellar. We would be warm for the long winter ahead.

Later in life I learned what dad meant when he remarked, "A man's word is his bond." It meant of course, when a person makes an oral commitment it became a binding promise to do something for another. It was a contract to perform. In my dad's world it was the honorable way to do business. In our world today it does not seem to carry the same weight of credibility.

Businesses, governments, the military, media, politicians, and sometimes church institutions often make promises they can't or never intend to fulfill. We, as individuals, are so fallible that we make promises to do something and fail to deliver. We may have the best of intentions but human weakness prevails. Worse yet, we may agree to perform but have no sincere intention of doing so. Contracts, vows, covenants, and solemn promises are constantly broken.

But there is only one person, who when He makes a promise or covenant, will always follow through. He will forever perform because HIS WORD IS HIS BOND! That man, of course, is Jesus Christ. No other individual in history could ever make that promise and none other than Christ will.

When we despair of the world's failure to keep their promises, when we question if a culture of truth any longer exists, and when we doubt that there is anyone whom we can completely trust, then is the time to recall Christ's sure and certain promise of eternal life. This belief that I will live forever in eternity after death has always sustained me. Be assured it will sustain you in your grief and pain at the passing of your loved one.

Remember Christ's promise: "I am the resurrection and the life; whoever believes in me, even if he dies, will live, and everyone who lives and believes in me will never die" (Jn 11:25).

That's the greatest promise that the world has ever heard...and He makes it to you today.

CONCLUSION

"How great and wonderful are your works, Lord God Almighty. Just and true are your ways, O King of the nations."
                                                    Rev 15:3

When I look back at the years that I, and the thousands of my fellow deacons have spent in loyal service to God I invoke the words of Isaiah: "I rejoice heartily in the Lord, in my God is the joy of my soul." It is my hope that in reading this book all the married, single, retired, and widowed deacons will have renewed their joy in being deacons. I feel I have not only spoken for myself but have proclaimed to all the singular joy deacons experience when we have "acted justly, loved tenderly and walked humbly with our God" (Mic 6:8). Most people will readily admit that they made many mistakes in their lives and have their share of regrets. I count myself in their number. I do not regret, however, that I did not make millions, become the CEO of a large corporation, or become a famous sports figure, playwright, or politician. I do regret that I have not loved enough, have not spread more joy, have not served others more often...but I pray there is still time left. I take great consolation, as should my fellow deacons, priests, and laity in the words of Archbishop Fulton J. Sheen, "It does not take much time to be a saint, it only takes much love."

APPENDIX

HOW OTHER DEACONS
EXPERIENCE AND MAINTAIN JOY
IN THEIR MINISTRY

Deacon James P. Walsh
Holy Innocents Parish, Neptune, NJ
Diocese of Trenton
Ordained: May 17, 1980

1. In what ways do I experience true joy in my various ministries?

Whenever I reach out to someone who is marginalized in some way including the elderly, lonely, ill or hungry, abused or abandoned, this is when I am given special grace to interact with them. Although, at times I can be on auto-pilot going in, my yearning to minister will frequently fill me with heartfelt joy and knowledge of God's Presence in me. I know then it is the Spirit of God working through me that feeds and carries me on.

2. What obstacles do I encounter in trying to maintain a joyful and positive attitude in my ministries?

All of my many weaknesses do their best to tire me and hold me back. At times they seem to have the upper hand, but with my prayer life along with the grace of confession and of Holy Orders I can usually maintain a positive attitude.

3. How do I handle these obstacles and what suggestions do I offer for my fellow deacons?

In addition to my responses above, I encourage them above all to be men of prayer.

Priorities will slip at times and will come again in proper order.

Deacon Thomas J. DiCanio
St. Catharine's Church, Holmdel, NJ
Diocese of Trenton
Ordained: May 12, 2007

1. In what ways do I experience true joy in my various ministries?

The Gospels were written not to give us faith; they were written so we can understand our faith.

My joy is to take this understanding and connect it to our everyday lives. I share in my ministries that God is always with us.

All the Catholic Church teaches is about positive choices. Sacred Scripture, the Ten Commandments, the Beatitudes, the Our Father; all the prayers and liturgy teach positive choices.

2. What obstacle do I encounter in trying to maintain a joyful and positive attitude in my ministries?

The main obstacles, especially for deacons who are still in the workforce, is fatigue. So, we need to create a "Sacred Space" to reflect, pray, and have quiet time. Mother Teresa, shares: "We need to find God and He cannot be found in noise and restlessness. God is a friend of silence. See how trees, flowers, grass grow in silence; see the stars, the moon and the sun, how they move in silence. We need the silence to be able to touch souls."

3. How do I handle these obstacles and what suggestions do I offer for my fellow deacons?

My "Sacred Space" is golf: God's green grass, the ball and me....

Deacon André JP Guillet, Director
Office of the Permanent Diaconate
Diocese of Charleston, SC
Ordained: May 4, 1985

1. In what ways do I experience true joy in my various ministries?

I am a deacon for almost 31 years and it is a real joy to be a servant of the people. Moving around because of work, I have been assigned to a few parishes and worked well with many pastors and priests that I have always respected, even if did not always agree with them.

I enjoy preaching once a month, connecting with all the people in the parish. I love doing preparation for a wedding, and it is a real joy to baptize children— especially my grandkids.

I feel blessed to help my brothers and sisters in Christ to get an annulment, and I experience joy when I am asked to bless their wedding.

As the director for the Diaconate of Charleston, I enjoy meeting my brother deacons and their wives.

Prison Ministry gives me the joy of bringing a bit of peace and affection to the incarcerated.

2. What obstacles do I encounter in trying to maintain a joyful and positive attitude in my ministries?

As the coordinator between priests and deacons there are always many things to do and not enough time to do them. I find that emails are very often misunderstood, and it is always better for me to either speak face to face or by phone.

3. How do I handle these obstacles and what suggestions do I offer for my fellow deacons?

Meeting on a regular basis with my brother deacons, having a wise and holy spiritual director, making the commitment to go on an annual silent retreat are ways to refresh and renew me. Being open to suggestions, working as a team, and including Christ in all meetings are very helpful.

Deacon Michael Lonie
St. Catherine Church, Holmdel, NJ
Diocese of Trenton
Ordained: May, 2009

1. In what ways do I experience true joy in my various ministries?

I experience great joy when something I've said, words Jesus puts into my mouth, or something I've done—a simple smile—helps make Jesus' presence real for people I encounter.

2. What obstacles do I encounter in trying to maintain a joyful and positive attitude in my ministries?

Being human (at least I think I am), I find that living the Gospel message every day and practicing what I preach is difficult. This is especially true when being a deacon conflicts with being a disciple.

3. How do I handle these obstacles and what suggestions do I offer for my fellow deacons?

I handle this obstacle by talking to Jesus all the time and listening to what He has to say, by reading and reflecting on Sacred Scripture and learning what He actually did, by not only asking, "What would Jesus do?" but by asking, "What did Jesus do?" Then I try my best to follow Him.

Deacon J. Michael East
Director of Deacons
Archdiocese of Indianapolis
Ordained: June 28, 2008

1. In what ways do I experience true joy in my various ministries?

I am able to find a sense of fulfillment in my ministry to the sick and dying as many of them do not have families to attend to their needs especially the spiritual way of preparing them for the end of their earthly lives.

I am also involved in a prison ministry which provides an opportunity to bring Christ to those who may not know Him or who have drifted away. This can help reinforce that they are not necessarily bad people but have encountered situations which have led to some bad choices.

2. What obstacles do I encounter in trying to maintain a joyful and positive attitude in my ministries?

Maintaining a balance between ministry and family life is my biggest challenge.

3. How do I handle these obstacles and what suggestions do I offer for my fellow deacons?

Keeping a strong prayer life is my best advice to myself as well as my fellow deacons. It also helps to maintain a regular diet of spiritual direction which helps me to find where God is in my ministry.

Deacon Christopher Hansen
Staff Deacon, Church of St. Catharine
Holmdel, NJ, Diocese of Trenton
Ordained: May 4, 2002

1. In what ways do I experience true joy in my various ministries?

Joy, to me, is the result of loving/caring engagement. It is usually unexpected, as in making a heart-to-heart connection with someone: whether joyfully preparing them for marriage or sharing their heartache at the loss of a loved one. Joy is the intersection of the call to service and His call to love.

2. What obstacles do I encounter in trying to maintain a joyful and positive attitude in my ministries?

The greatest obstacle to a positive, joyful attitude is expectation. Any encounter that is begun with a personal level of expectation can result in disappointment. I love our God of surprises. Each of His surprises can be an opportunity for joy if I allow it to be.

3. How do I handle these obstacles and what suggestions do I offer for my fellow deacons?

Prayer, before, during, and after the ministerial opportunities God presents me is the essential ingredient for joy in ministry. As ministry does not always provide me with the opportunity to pray in anticipation of service, the office of deacon calls me to pray always, sometimes using words.

Deacon Michael Ghiorso
Our Lady of Mercy Church
Archdiocese of San Francisco
Ordained: June 19, 2005

1. In what ways do I experience true joy in my various ministries?

I experience joy in many different aspects of my ministry but true joy is most noticeably present to me in the Sacrament of Baptism. I believe it is the welcoming of new members, bundled with the wonder of new families and our church community coming together in celebration and thanksgiving. There is something about this "sacred moment" (Sacrament) that transcends all other events and ministry.

2. What obstacles do I encounter in trying to maintain a joyful and positive attitude in my ministries?

As with most vocations and ministry, deacons are worn down by the day-to-day minutiae. We must accomplish all the things we "have to do" before we get to the work we want to do. When ministers hear the discouraging words: "We don't do that here," both we and our communities suffer because we fail to be open to the possibilities of change and improvement. But, even in these moments, I find God working on my attitude and convincing me that, just maybe, this situation is exactly where I am supposed to be.

3. How do I handle these obstacles and what suggestions do I offer for my fellow deacons?

I usually turn to spiritual reading, Scripture, deacon-friends and, most notably, my wife when I battle "the blues." I am fortunate to have a great deal of support from all these sources, and I am capable of returning to my retreats, homilies, and teaching revitalized by their care. The joy remains in the work, and I take that as a sure sign of God's grace.

Deacon Francis B. Orlando
Archdiocese of New York
Director of Diaconate Formation
Ordained: June 24, 1989 by John Cardinal O'Connor

1. In what ways do I experience true joy in my various ministries?

I experience joy when I am able to bring a sense of joy to others. It fills me with joy when I explain Scripture or an Article of Faith and I see a spark of understanding in the eyes of just one person in the group. I experience joy when I baptize an infant and I see the joy and the pride of the new parents. When I witness a wedding I am grateful to experience the joy of being with a couple, united in Christ, who are about to embark on a great journey.

Whether teaching, preaching, administering the sacraments, or simply sitting with a person who is in a troubled state of mind, I find great joy in the knowledge that I am where God wants me to be.

2. What obstacles do I encounter in trying to maintain a joyful and positive attitude in my ministries?

Among the very few obstacles is the attitude of those who see the Church only in the light of the scandals reported in the media. My joyfulness is diminished because these unfortunate people, are deprived of the true joy that is the Catholic faith. Even more, the very thought that there were people within the Church who did commit unthinkable acts, saps me of joy.

3. How do I handle these obstacles and what suggestions do I offer for my fellow deacons?

For me there is only one way to handle these obstacles to joy—that is to stay close to Jesus in prayer and in the Sacraments. We cannot do what we are ordained to do without a close and personal relationship with Our Savior. Jesus is our source of strength, joy, and peace. Without Him we can do nothing; with Him everything is possible.

BIBLIOGRAPHY

Callahan, Sidney. *Created for Joy-A Christian View of Suffering*. The Crossword Publishing Co., New York, NY, 2007.

Catoir, Rev. John. *That Your Joy May Be Full*. The Christophers, New York, NY, 1982.

Joyfully Living the Gospel Day by Day. Catholic Book Publishing, Corp., Totowa, NJ, 2011.

Champlin, Rev. Joseph M. *The Joy of Being an Altar Server*. Catholic Book Publishing Corp., Resurrection Press, Totowa, NJ, 2002.

Damico, Rev. Rod. *The Joy of Preaching-Embracing the Gift and Promise*. Catholic Book Publishing Corp./ Resurrection Press, Totowa, NJ, 2001.

De Caussade, Jean-Pierre. *The Joy of Full Surrender*. Paraclete Press, Brewster, MA, 2011.

Ditewig, Deacon William T. *The Deacon At Mass: A Theological Pastoral Guide*. Paulist Press, Mahwah, NJ, 2007.

Downey, Michael. *The New Dictionary of Catholic Spirituality*, The Liturgical Press, Collegeville, MN, 1993.

Finley, Mitch. *The Joy of Being a Eucharistic Minister*. Catholic Book Publishing Corp., Resurrection Press, Totowa, NJ, 1998.

The Joy of Being a Lector. Catholic Book Publishing Corp., Resurrection Press, Totowa, NJ, 2000.

Flanagan, John P. *Managing Your Time, Energy and*

Talent in Ministry. St. Paul/ Alba House, Staten Island, NY, 2006.

Flynn, Leslie. *The Gift of Joy–God Wants You in His Joy Explosion*. Victor Books, Wheaton, IL, 1980.

Kelly, Matthew. *A Call to Joy–Living in the Presence of God*. San Francisco, CA, 1997.

Lewis, C.S. *The Joyful Christian*. Macmillan Publishing Co., New York, NY, 1977.

Peale, Norman Vincent. *Treasury of Joy and Enthusiasm.* K.S. Giniger Co., New York, NY, 1979.

Phelps, Owen. *The Catholic Vision for Leading Like Jesus*. Our Sunday Visitor, Huntington, IN, 2008.

Pope Francis. *The Joy of the Gospel-Evangelii Gaudium* (Apostolic Exhortation). Washington, D.C. U.S.C.C.B., 2013 Liberia Editrice Vaticana, Vatican City, Rome.

Rossetti, Stephen J. *A Study of the Psychological and Spiritual Health of Priests*. Ave Maria Press, Notre Dame, IN, 2011.

Samra, Cal. *The Joyful Christ–The Healing Power of Humor.* Harper Collins Publishing, New York, NY, 1986.

St. Romain, Philip. *Pathways to Serenity*, Liguori Publications, Liguori, MO, 1988.

Wiersbe, Warren W. *Be Joyful–It Beats Being Happy*. *Victor Books*, Wheaton, IL, 1978.

Wirt, Sherwood E. *Jesus, Man of Joy*. Harvest Home Publishers, Eugene, OR, 1999.